Turn Your Wounds into Wings

BOOK ONE
HEALING

Five Weeks to Becoming Resilient in Love
Healing from Past Relationships Through Self-Love
and Awaken Your Heart to the Love Around You

New York

Cataloging-in-Publication Data is on file at the Library of Congress

ISBN: 978-1-7341838-8-7 (print)
ISBN: 978-1-7341838-7-0 (e-book)

Printed in the United States

Dedication

To my mom, my greatest hero and role model, who teaches me how to be happy and strong with grace, kindness, love, and laughter.

To Gabby Bernstein, my teacher and mentor, without whom this book and the person I am today would not be.

And to her husband, Zach. What an amazing team you guys are.

Thank you both for your love, compassion and support.

What You Can Expect
from This Book

This book will help you:

✓ Heal your wounds from past relationships following the guidelines in this book to make you resilient in love.

✓ Help you understand there is a meaning and purpose for the relationships that come into your life.

✓ Help you let go of painful stories from the past that are lowering your self-worth, and holding you back from the love you want and deserve.

✓ Finally let go of that partner who keeps you enmeshed in a heartbreaking relationship.

✓ Learn how to heal, honor and value yourself by setting a firm foundation through the practice of self-love.

✓ Learn how to live wholeheartedly single, so you can enjoy your life right now even without a partner.

✓ Learn that your self-worth is not tied to having a partner.

✓ Learn what blocks your happiness and how to set yourself free.

✓ Open your heart to the abundance of love that is already all around you.

✓ Learn how to live a more meaningful, inspired life.

Table of Contents

Love Letter
1

Introduction
9

My Story
13

Dating Detox
35

Your Personal Growth Toolkit
43

Lesson One
The Childhood Wound (Optional)
49

Lesson Two
Forgiveness
Letting Go/Non-Attachment/Acceptance
67

Lesson Three
Self-Forgiveness/Self-Compassion
109

Lesson Four
Self-Love/Self-Care
Being Wholeheartedly Single
151

Lesson Five
Love is Everywhere
201

A Love Letter
from Me to You

ESILIENT LOVE is a book, a program, and a journey so close to my heart, because it is my heart. The lessons and exercises in this book come from my own personal healing journey going through a divorce, which resulted in a major life change that led me to leave a twenty-year career in public relations and special events and become a transformational life coach. This journey completely changed my life, and it can do the same for you, if you allow it. That is the purpose of the journey: To continue to learn and grow.

Life is your school. Experience your lessons. Teachers are only here to help guide you along the path, but it is up to you to start and stay on the journey, and in which direction you choose to go, but no one can walk the path for you. You are the captain, the creator of your life. You determine what you allow into your journey (and even what you resist). On these pages, you will discover what I learned from my teachers—the ones I chose, along with the teachers I didn't choose; the ones sent to me by the Universe in my everyday life, to put what I learned into practice, and who helped me to see how our perception of love, (or mostly our fear of love), affects our relationships, our lives, and our view of the world.

When we become disillusioned about love because of the past, or through our limiting beliefs, self-judgment, and expectations—stress, anxiety, and depression set in, and our relationships and daily lives begin to suffer. We say we want to be happy, but we do so much to keep ourselves unhappy. In truth, I saw how I was creating a lot of my

own suffering, but acknowledging it is what helped me to become free of how I was sabotaging myself.

You know when you discover something really good, and you want to share it with everyone? The lessons in this book were my roadmap to freedom, and I want to share them with all of you. Some of these concepts may be new to you, so try to keep an open mind. Take what works for you, and let go of whatever isn't working for you right now.

Initially, I geared this book towards women, but as I started sharing more on social media, I noticed a lot of men were reaching out to me after reading my posts or listening to a podcast interview I had done. They expressed to me how much this work was helping them. This helped to open my eyes to the growing need for men who were also seeking healing in their lives, and in this world. This book can certainly help men, as well as anyone in the LGBTQ+ community, find the healing they need, because love and truth do not know gender or race. Love does not discriminate. Underneath our unique exteriors, we are all the same, souls looking for love, acceptance, healing and peace.

We all have been wounded in some way. Whether it was by a partner, friend, relative, or a parent. No one in this world has been spared. We can either learn from what happened to us to better our lives, or we can be defined by our trauma and allow it to control our lives. There is a need for deep healing of the souls in this world that are living and reacting from their wounds. Protecting your heart in relationships and in the world can be exhausting, and can leave us feeling lost, lonely, angry, resentful, or confused. There must be another way? Resilient Love, a series of two books, gives you permission to disarm and open yourself up to finding love and empowerment within yourself, showing you that the light inside of you is more powerful than any walls you can build around you to protect you.

You are about to embark on a deep, beautiful journey of healing, self-love, empowerment, and freedom. Freedom from what hurt you, made you feel unloved, and unworthy. You were led to this book because you are ready. Something intuitively is telling you that there's more, and something has to change. That nagging feeling is your soul's way of trying to guide you in the right direction. That is your intuition, and it's up to you whether you will listen to it. The problem for most of us is that we were never taught how to use our intuition for guidance, so we don't know how to listen to it. We ignore it. We drown out our intuition with constant mind chatter or with some type of distraction, like TV or music. We hate to be alone with ourselves and our thoughts. Avoidance has become our default, not wanting to face what we are feeling, so how can we hear when our soul is trying to get our attention?

Or worse yet, we believe our ego, which is our fears and our false self, and we follow our wounds over our soul's guidance. Until you wake up and become aware, many of you won't trust what your soul is trying to tell you. Because the soul speaks from the heart, and ego thinks that's weakness. It makes us feel too vulnerable and afraid. Ego likes to feel strong, but ego will always lure us into a false sense of empowerment through blame, force, resentment, payback—and all their petty ways—further distancing us from the very love we want. But ego's small, prideful, and fearful ways will try to tell you, "Who needs love?"

Let's get one thing straight; love does not hurt. It's people who do not know how to love that cause hurt. However, if you keep ignoring your soul's guidance towards what love really is, and how it all begins and ends within you and not in someone or something else, the Universe will continue to send you signs and lessons until you understand. Often, by that point, we are down on our knees, begging and searching for help, and for many of you, that is how you wound up here, searching for answers, searching for healing, searching for growth. That's how I wound up here. "Hello!"

It's important to understand that the Universe is not trying to punish you. Actually, we punish ourselves by not listening and resisting. The Universe is simply sending you a clear message to guide you in the right direction, the direction that will set you free from yourself.

We humans don't seem to get the message until we are hit over the head with it many times; sometimes many, many, many, times. Until we finally come to understand it is in the pain and difficulties of life that we can find the lesson and gain wisdom. It's when you experience heartbreak in a relationship. You can't see it in the middle of your pain, but there are treasures to be found in the lessons; for example, the lesson that someone who didn't see your worth can

show you how to stand up for yourself and find your worth. You begin to understand that all things, even the difficulties, are there to work out for your own good, and everything that happened to you led you to exactly where you need to be for the next step in your evolution. Had it not happened, you would not be where you are now.

Some of my worst pains turned into my greatest lessons, which helped me to stop blaming others for my choices. Instead, I started taking responsibility, honoring and loving myself more, and made better choices that served my highest good. This is the true meaning of empowerment: When you take responsibility for your life, and your choices, you claim your power.

This is the beginning of being awakened to awareness. Awakening is when you start becoming aware that your past does not define you, but that your life has been a culmination of your choices. Awareness helps us to understand why things happened the way they did and how everything interacts and reacts to one another (cause and effect), so we can choose to try to create better outcomes instead of leaving everything to fate or on another person to fix or handle.

The lessons we learn through our awareness are what help us heal from the past and the false stories we have accepted as truth, until now. Stories we tell ourselves, that we are not good enough, are unlovable, are unworthy. Freedom begins when we stop believing in our limiting beliefs and learn how to trust the journey and the Universe.

Even if you haven't found the cause or the reason for the lesson, you still trust it was meant to be. Becoming aware of what is happening within you and around you is known as "expansion." Think of it as widening your scope. Expansion means more freedom. Freedom from how we create our own suffering. You feel freer and lighter from the egoic thoughts that were once weighing you down. Once you know what that freedom feels like, freedom from how you sabotage yourself from peace and happiness, keeping your peace becomes the biggest priority.

Most everything in life is about seeking love, either negatively or positively. Searching negatively is when we seek to fill the emptiness (absence of love) with drugs, sex, alcohol, or food. When we seek love in positive ways, we seek love through our connection to the divine through meditation, prayer, yoga, intention, creating, serving others—anything that inspires us, feeds the soul, and lights us up. Seeking love negatively leads to more retreating, isolation, depression, and another fix. Seeking love in positive ways leave us feeling more fulfilled, more loving, more generous, more kind, more inspired, more alive.

As a transformational spiritual life coach and teacher, part of my work is to teach people how to have that "ah-ha" moment sooner, rather than staying stuck, frustrated, and unhappy. Kind of like one of those experts who give you life-hacks for your home or cooking, which make your life easier. A life coach provides you with life-hacks for your mental well-being, which makes your life feel easier, lighter, happier with more meaning and joy. I help move my clients forward by teaching them how to listen to their own teacher and guidance within. All the answers already exist within you; I just show you how to tap into them.

This book is designed to help you open up and expand your mindset, so you can have a higher level of awareness. It's time for you to stop walking around aimlessly, in pain about yourself and your relationships, which for the most part, is what you will continue to do until you understand how the Universe works when it comes to relationships. This is your guide and toolkit to help you navigate your course and bring more clarity, happiness, meaning, and love into your life.

Many people say they want change, but few are willing to go through the difficult process to make that change happen. You may know someone who fits that description. You may have been that person yourself. However, something has shifted in you, and you've decided you want to make that change now. That is huge! Just by reading this book, you are showing the Universe your willingness to change. You are making a pact with yourself to grow and heal. That in itself is a declaration of self-love and honoring yourself.

I also know many of you reading this book are not new to this path. You know exactly what I have been talking about so far. This book may just be the next step in your journey. Maybe you came onto this path through helping people heal their career or money fears, or maybe you help people heal through health coaching, as reiki master, or a yoga teacher. Healing relationships is just the next step in your process. No one is ahead or behind on this path. We all grow

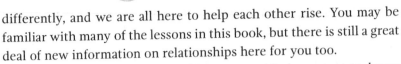

differently, and we are all here to help each other rise. You may be familiar with many of the lessons in this book, but there is still a great deal of new information on relationships here for you too.

For those who are new to this process, it's important to know this is not "self-improvement," as you have nothing that you need to improve. We're doing quite the opposite. We're deconstructing the layers of false beliefs that keep us in judgment of ourselves. Believing we are flawed and not good enough is how many of us wound up here in the first place. Low self-esteem and self-worth can lead to unhealthy relationships. Looking for the love we lack for ourselves in someone else can, more often than not, lead you into relationships with people who do not have your best interest in mind. Not loving yourself could also lead you to sabotage your relationships, because you don't believe that someone could love you for who you really are, when that is the furthest thing from the truth. The personal transformation and spiritual growth paths help to undo those beliefs that make us feel like we are not good enough so we can learn to love and accept ourselves as the beautifully imperfect human beings we are. Remarkedly this also helps us to raise our standards for better relationships, and be attracted to better partners, as we become wiser, and better partners ourselves.

You can't cheat on a personal development or spiritual path. Sure, you can skip over pages in this book, but you cannot skip or runaway from a universal lesson. You'll know this when you keep repeating the same heartbreaking or frustrating situations, over and over again. You either wind up in another painful heartbreaking relationship, or you keep going back to the same heartbreaking painful relationship. It is because you have not yet learned what it is trying to teach you. You cannot pass a lesson until you understand why it is being presented to you.

So, it's important not to skip any lessons in this book, because they are designed to help you understand how to work with the universal lessons coming up in your life. However, you can definitely skip an exercise if it does not pertain to your situation.

The words I have written on these pages are what I came to realize is my life's purpose—to help release people from their suffering and awaken their hearts to love again. It is through the practices on these pages that I have been able to become resilient in love, and so can you. All you need to do is keep an open mind, stay committed, and show up—not for me, but for yourself, every day. All God and the Universe want for all of us is love, peace, and happiness, but we keep getting in the way.

If you continue on this path, you will evolve and grow, you will come to learn that there is no competition in spiritual development. You don't become more spiritual or enlightened than someone else, but rather you become more understanding and compassionate of others. You don't push yourself, as much as you allow—and things happen naturally in divine order.

Expanding your awareness helps you see things not as you want to see them, but it helps you see things as they really are. As you heal your inner world and grow, the developmental changes show up in your outer world, especially in your relationship with others, and more importantly, the relationship you have with yourself. Nothing has really changed in your world, only the way you see it. Things will get brighter, and you'll find more magic, meaning, and love in your life. This is my wish for you and everyone in this world: To be happy and free and find more love, magic, meaning, and miracles in their lives. To heal and release your wounds by lighting the torch from within and passing that light onto others.

Together we can help heal and illuminate the world.

Namaste,
The light in me honors the light in you.

Karen OM

Introduction

ESILIENT LOVE: TURN YOUR Wounds into Your Wings: Healing from Past Relationships Through Self-Love is the first book of a two-part series. You can do this course on your own, with a friend, a group of friends, or a book club. You can also join the online Facebook group, "Resilient Love Book Club." It is a closed community for our members' privacy to keep the integrity of the group, so please include the code, "Resilient Lover" in your message for access. When you do a self-study course with a friend or a group, there is always support and commitment present, which is like having a running buddy. You will be able to ask questions or share your "ah-ha" moments from the book with others on the same journey.

This book, just as with many other spiritual or personal trans-formation books, will provide different results for each person who reads it. The reader always seems to get the exact message they need to receive. Much like *A Course in Miracles*, which has an almost magical ability to touch, heal, and send love to whatever part of your soul is in need. Works like *A Course in Miracles* can only be the work of the divine. I tell you, no matter where you are in your spiritual beliefs—whether you believe in God, walked away from church years ago or never had a relationship with a higher power—you are meant to be here. All are accepted and welcome here.

This book is also the combination of my interpretation of my teach-ers and mentors teachings, such as, Gabby Bernstein (*The Universe Has Your Back*); the principles of *A Course in Miracles*; Deepak Cho-pra (*The Seven Spiritual Laws of Success*); Brenè Brown (*The Power of*

Vulnerability); Marianne Williamson (*A Return to Love*); Oprah Winfrey; Tara Brach (*Radical Acceptance*); and Kristen Neff (*Self-Compassion*), along with my dedicated practice and love of yoga. As you explore and expand your own path, you will also be drawn to many of your own books and teachers. There are so many paths on this journey from Buddhism to the yoga sutras, mindfulness, meditation, and many more teachers such as Lao Tsu, Eckart Tolle, Pema Chödrön, Wayne Dyer, and Yogi Bhajan, to only name a few. I believe God, the Universe, created all these paths because he knew we are all so different, so he spoke through many teachers and created many different paths to reach us, so we could find our way back home.

We may be drawn to different teachers and styles of teaching, but the messages are the all same, "love one another," "peace begins with you," "do not judge," "be kind," "have faith," "do not fear," "trust," and "believe." Most spirituality practices teach mindfulness as the most beneficial tool to help clear our thoughts and stay connected to peace, love, and guidance of God, and the Universe.

~ ~ ~

When I first started writing this book, it was designed to be a workbook with eight lessons for my clients. I thought it would be a paragraph with a couple of exercises after each lesson. However, something was guiding me to write, and more than I ever imagined came pouring out of me onto these pages, and my little workbook evolved into a book. I hadn't known it was a book at the time, not until my friend Rachel who was helping me to edit my book came back to me and said, "This isn't a workbook, Karen. It's a book! Your book!" I didn't think I was ready to write a book, but at more than two hundred pages, it was no longer a workbook, but an actual book.

I wanted to test the comprehension and exercises of the workbook with beta testers before launching it. The first group of beta testers said they were enjoying the workbook and benefitting from the lessons. The first part of the book was healing, and the second part of the book was moving forward. The only negative feedback they reported was that it was a lot of work. It is work, but it is also important work. Another tester spoke up and said she was not ready to move forward.

And everyone agreed that future groups would appreciate a break after healing, and before moving forward onto the final lessons. Thus, the book was divided into two books, "Healing" and "Moving Forward."

I had wanted to launch it as one book, because I feared that some readers would bypass the first book, not wanting to do the healing work, and just move onto the second book, since it talks about gaining the ability to "recognize the right partners." I feared they would not get the complete benefit of the entire work. However, I started seeing more people who were not ready to move forward into a new relationship. They wanted to heal from the last relationship and stay single for a little while.

Sure, there are some people who want to move forward and heal their pain by jumping into another relationship, which is not the healthiest or best way to meet the right partner, especially if they have a history of bad relationships, but either way, I realized I could not control what people want to do or how they choose to do it, so I agreed to divide this work into two books. I let go of how I wanted it to be. I knew that the people ready to do the work would do the work.

I then re-tested the first book with another group of beta testers who were not familiar with coaching or a spiritual practice and without weekly coaching sessions with me, as the first group had received. I wanted to see how they received it; just as a reader would be purchasing this book online. The results were equally as amazing. They understood the work. One woman, just as in the first group, was finally able to end an unhealthy on-again-off-again relationship that was going nowhere, but still keep her heart open to love. Other women said they had less fear around dating and were more open to love, while feeling more empowered being single than ever before. I was already feeling this work was accomplishing what I had hoped, and it wasn't even published yet. Even more amazing, this work was bringing out what each woman needed to heal so they could move forward, just as it had done for me.

If you are new to personal transformation or a spiritual practice, don't let the word "spiritual" freak you out. The term "spiritual practice" refers to anything you do that nurtures and enlightens your soul, and it will help you greatly to understand that this is just the beginning of an ongoing practice. You can't expect to read a book or take a workshop, and your life will be completely transformed. You may feel enlightened and energized afterward, but then a few weeks go by, old behaviors creep back in, and it's life as usual. In order to have a long-lasting or even permanent effect, you have to practice every day. Which is why keeping your practice simple and sticking to what you love and enjoy will make you more likely to return to it. You will grab your yoga mat to go release and surrender more than you will grab a glass of wine to escape.

Eventually, making it a practice, you don't know how you lived without it for so long. There is not a day that goes by that I don't say, "I am so grateful for this practice. What a gift this has been." I will give you simple tools to use in your everyday life. I will also tell you: You will get out of this program what you put in. Just like a dancer or a gymnast, practicing once a week or once a month is going to reflect much differently than if you practice every day. You are building a muscle, and using that muscle every day will make it stronger. Don't let the word "practice" throw you off either. Practice in spiritual terms is more about surrender, release, acceptance, forgiveness, non-judgment, compassion, and kindness. Once you get in the flow, practice; just like breathing, it will become second nature to you.

I will also be using the words, "spirit," "God," and the "Universe" throughout this book. These words are whatever they mean to you. Don't let these words turn you away from what you can get out of this book. They are here to help you align with your definition of what your higher power is and what it means to you. Even if your higher power is your intuition, that's perfect. This is a safe judgement-free zone.

If you read something that does not resonate with you, take what does work for you and leave behind what does not. Don't throw out something in its entirety simply because one thing did not resonate with you. Take what does work for you and cultivate it. If you only get one important thing out of this book that you didn't have before you read it, then it served its purpose. But for the rest of you, may the lessons in this book change your life as they did mine.

~ ~ ~

My Story
Divorce and Awakening

ILWAUKEE, WISCONSIN. IT'S A beautiful fall day. I'm sitting in my car in the mall parking lot in front of Barnes & Noble, and I'm a mess. I'm going through a divorce after twelve years of marriage. My life coach, Anna, is available 24/7, but I don't want to bother her on her day off, especially not on such a gorgeous day. I keep vacillating on whether this divorce is the right thing. And feeling like, "I have to get the hell out of here now. I can't take it here a minute longer." I feel like I'm in limbo. Neither here nor there. Not really married, but not fully divorced either. I'm in Milwaukee, but all I want is to be is back in my hometown of New York City with my family and friends. But then what? What will happen to me once I get back to New York? Unless you've done the dance of indecisive limbo, you don't know how utterly torturous it can be. I just wanted everything to be over and behind us but I was terrified to get there.

Do you need to know all the gory details of our marriage? If this were a memoir maybe, but as someone who's read a lot of self-help books while I was in crisis, all I wanted to know was, "Did you make it? And if so, tell me how you did it. Maybe it will help me too."

Anyone who has been through a divorce, especially when you have been together for as long as we had been, will agree—it is one of the hardest things you will ever go through in your life. Many couples stay together out of fear. Fear of being alone after divorce. Fear of their financial condition after the divorce. For me, there was a lot of fear around, "What is going to happen to me? Who am I going

to be after my life with this person for nearly nineteen years?" My identity had been wrapped around my husband, especially after we transferred from New York (where we met) to Chicago due to his job, and later moving to Milwaukee to be closer to his family.

I found myself terrified, wondering, "How will I get my life back together again after so many years? I'll have to get a new job and a new place. This time on my own." Just like when we came to the Midwest, but in reverse. Undoing everything. "And how am I going to get all my stuff back?" It all seemed so daunting that just the thought of it made me hyperventilate, so I kept pushing it back and kept pushing it back. We had tried to make it work for many years, but we couldn't see eye-to-eye on most anything, and now we were living completely separate lives. He, vacationing up at his cabin, and me, back in New York City.

I now know, I was in classic "victim mode," which is when someone's mindset leads them to believe they are completely helpless, sometimes to the point they become hopeless. Victim mode is debilitating. You can't see past your fears no matter how ridiculous they may be. It's like that meme of the horse tied to a plastic chair and the caption reads, "Sometimes what's stopping you is all in your head." In my mind, I couldn't move back, because I didn't know how to get all my stuff back to New York. Seriously, that's how bad victim mode was for me. Of course, it's completely ridiculous. Obviously, I made it back, but at the time, it really was too daunting for me.

"Just hire a moving truck." I know, many of you are thinking that it should have been easy right? But there was a lot more than that going on. Then again, there wasn't. Fear is a filter, and in this instance, it was making everything appear overwhelming. Fear can leave us stuck, having a firm psychological grip on you if you allow it. We each have our own ridiculous fears to deal with in this life, so you can't mock someone else's. What's easy for you may be difficult for someone else and vice versa. When you are in a victim mindset, you are fixated on the blocks; you can't see a way around them.

During my marriage, I had also gone through the most incredibly tough years of my life with my family back in New York. My dad fell ill from kidney failure, only a few months after our wedding. I flew back and forth often to help care for him. He had always been out and about his entire life, trotting all over the world as a liaison between American and Japanese businesses, always involved in a new project, and now he was like a caged bird. He lived like this for eight years, until early one morning my phone rang; it was my oldest sister Marjorie calling to tell me our father had passed away. It was my first experience with death and grief. Everything seemed surreal, like a nightmare from which I couldn't wake up. His death, coupled with the difficulties in my marriage and deciding to leave an incredibly stressful job, left me at home, jobless and in grief. I fell into a deep depression with terrible anxiety. I did whatever I could to get back on my feet again, because I was damned if that was going to be my life.

I was not going to live that way. Then, just as I was getting back on my feet again, I received another early morning phone call (God, how I was really beginning to hate these early morning phone calls). The voice on the other end of the line—I don't even recall who it was—told me Marjorie had passed away from a diabetic-related stroke. Four years after my father had passed. At that moment, all the healing I had worked so hard towards vanished; I felt my life and my world as I knew it crumbling around me. My mother, who was getting up there in years, was now all alone in New York. The closest relative was my only other sister living in Washington, DC.

Things never seemed to get back on par between my husband and me; if anything, they were probably worse. Like a grinding wheel slowly wearing away at our marriage. I was so frustrated with myself for not being able to take the leap and file for a divorce. I felt like a big talker. It was easy to say, "I want to divorce," but so much harder to put into action. I was on the phone with my friend Tamar in New York, bitching about my life. Tamar, who was also going through a divorce, suggested I speak with a therapist.

"Interview at least three," she said, "to find a good fit," and that is how I found my life coach Anna. Anna was an attractive, well-dressed blonde haired woman about my age, also divorced. She felt like someone who would understand what I was going through, and more importantly, help me get out of my own way. When I hired Anna, I told her, "Your job is to help me get to the other side," (by which, I meant New York), "and to file for a divorce. Because I know I am going to back out, and if I don't do this, I am going to hate myself for

the rest of my life." The feeling of whether what I was doing was the right thing still wasn't going away.

As I write this, I realize how accustomed we get to feeling unhappy. We get so used to feeling bad and believing life is "good enough," until it becomes acceptable to feel life is simply mediocre, "This is just how life is." Constantly complaining about how much life sucks to our friends. Blinded to the fact that there could be another way. That's the victim's view of life. Even if someone points the way, we can't see it. We'll tell them they don't understand, but really, we're staying with what we know, where it feels safe. "I may be miserable, but at least I know what to expect. God forbid (here comes the New Yorker in me), I should take a risk and be happy. Smart people know better, risks are for crazy people." We see other people who are happy and think that it's luck or that some people are "just happy." Or worse, we believe other people's happiness is fake, rather than realizing it's a choice. However, choosing happiness can sometimes come with huge life changes, such as leaving a marriage or a job you are unhappy with, or starting the business of your dreams. Some people move through this effortlessly, while others remain stuck. However, everything you really want or dream about is outside of that comfort zone. Had I not been pushed to the edge, I probably would have continued to live my life in a state of misery, believing it was normal. And that is the purpose of being pushed to the edge: To wake you up.

After the divorce was over, my ex (we are actually pretty good friends now, probably because we don't live together or have to make any major life decisions together anymore), called one day to say our beloved Anabelle was dying. Anabelle was our sixteen-year-old grey-and-white tuxedo rescue cat. She was my cat, my best friend and confidant, for many sad and lonely years. I left Anabelle with him, because she had a big house with lots of windows where she could stare out at the chipmunks and the squirrels that kept her entertained every day. In New York, she would be cooped up in a sixth-floor apartment that overlooked other buildings. I didn't think it was fair to relocate her after so many years. I also didn't want my ex to come home to an empty house. My ex and I weren't suited for one another; I didn't feel the need to punish him. I made him promise me if I left Anabelle with him, he would let me know if anything happened to her, and the dreaded call came at 11:00 p.m., two years after our divorce was final.

"Anabelle is sick. I don't know how much longer she has, Karen." I jumped on a plane two days later. I was surprised, but also relieved she was still hanging in there so I could say, "Good-bye." Five days later, and she was still barely hanging on each day. Friends of mine told me she was most likely still alive because she was so excited to see me, even though she was clearly suffering. She was still fluffy and beautiful, but when I picked her up, she was nothing but skin and bones. She winced and let out a small cry when I cradled her in my arms. Every breath was a struggle.

On the last morning, my ex was at work in Chicago, I sat on my old couch in Milwaukee, cradling Anabelle in my arms. I quietly whispered in her ear, "Mama loves you so much, sweetie. It's so wonderful seeing you again, but I can see you are in so much pain. It's okay to go, sweetie. I'll meet you on the other side, okay?" And I kissed her on the forehead. Shortly after, Anabelle took her last breath, I kissed her again, and she passed away in my arms.

My ex said he was grateful I came back for Anabelle. He couldn't take off work, and he didn't want her to die alone. She didn't deserve that; she was too special to us. I decided to stay a few more days and drive up with him to the family cabin on the lake, one last time, together. We had a nice quiet dinner at the local supper club. We returned to the cabin, and I remember my ex calling me outside. I went outside, and he said, "Lookup" and he turned off the front cabin lights. I remember looking up in the pitch black sky and through the tall evergreen trees, I saw a gazillion stars. My heart ached, but it was so awe-inspiringly beautiful, one of the most bittersweet magical moments of my life. Something made me feel Anabelle was happy to see her parents getting along in this moment.

We returned inside and comfortably adjourned to separate rooms. The next morning after breakfast, we laid Anabelle to rest next to his childhood dog and a few other family pets. I was happy Anabelle wasn't alone. There would be other family pets to keep her company. Then, like old times, my ex and I argued. This time about why I needed music for Anabelle's funeral. Why couldn't it just be

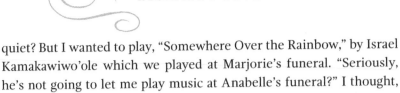
quiet? But I wanted to play, "Somewhere Over the Rainbow," by Israel Kamakawiwo'ole which we played at Marjorie's funeral. "Seriously, he's not going to let me play music at Anabelle's funeral?" I thought, "You can't divorce someone twice, can you?"

He reluctantly let me play the song as we lowered her down in the beautiful tapestry box I purchased for our home before the divorce. I never imagined at the time I purchased it to hide travel brochures in the living room, that I would be burying Anabelle in it, one day. My ex later apologized, after liking my music selection and said it was a nice funeral. We returned to Milwaukee later that afternoon, so I could catch my flight back to New York. We had a little time before my flight, so we sat out on our old front porch together.

The topic of the end of our marriage came up. I told him, I hated saying that my reason for the divorce was because "I wanted to be happy." That sounded so selfish, and it didn't ring true to what I was feeling. I explained it to him, "It's not that I wanted to be 'happy,' I just didn't want to be 'unhappy' anymore." He lowered his head, nodded, and told me he understood. He told me my coming back brought a lot peace and closure for him. I was grateful for this moment.

When the divorce had finalized, I took my portion of the settlement, bought myself a decent used car. My old car was my dad's old car I inherited after he passed away. I couldn't even trade it in; it was so old, they demolished it. And after a twenty-year career in PR, marketing, and special events, I went back to school to get my certification as a life coach. This wasn't a midlife crisis. A midlife crisis would have been a brand-new sports car, boob job, and a vacation in Mexico. Instead, this was a rebirth. Life can bring you to your knees, and some people do everything they can to escape the pain, by going out and drinking with friends and dating excessively. For other people, it's isolating themselves and numbing the pain with Netflix and comfort food. But for the few, when life brings you to your knees, you go *into* the pain to heal it, and it becomes your wake-up call.

So how did I get from there to here? Well, it all started that beautiful fall day in the mall parking lot in front of Barnes & Noble. I had finally summoned up the courage to talk to my husband about divorce with the help of my life coach, Anna. However, what no one tells you is that even when you want a divorce, it isn't easy. Honestly, if you are having doubts about leaving a marriage or relationship, I don't think there is any book that is going to give you the confidence you need to make you feel like you are 100% doing the right thing, and not leave you with any doubt. It's something where you have to take the leap and get to the other side of the divorce. And even then, it's not over. The doubt finally went away for me after the divorce, but in its place was heartache and healing from the breakup itself. No one really wants a divorce. They wanted it to work; that's why they got married. They only got to divorce, because it didn't work out.

I had read so many books on divorce, trying to find the answer on whether it was right for me, as I said none of them gave me the confidence I needed, except for one book I came across called, *Choosing Me Before We*, by Christine Arylo. What the book did was help me understand that I didn't know how to pick a partner who was right for me in the first place? The book wasn't about divorce. It was more of a book you would read before you got married.

In the book, Christine talks about how we use romantic love to fill the empty voids within us. I had never heard of this concept before, and it resonated deeply with me. I could see how we build our idea of relationships on this premise of it filling up the loneliness within us. We actually think that the purpose of relationships is to fill up those wounds and make us happy when that is not the purpose at all. And most likely why so many of us are screwing it up and why the divorce rate is so high. It's probably one of the worst reasons to get married, along with being pressured into it, doing it for money, pregnancy, to make your parents happy, or because you want a wedding. I wish I had known about this when I was in high school, even junior high school, when all my thoughts were about love and the belief that someday, Prince Charming would come to save me and make me happy. Those fairytales mess us up a lot. Christine talked about how self-love is the antidote to fill the voids within ourselves, another concept with which I was not familiar. What was this self-love? I wanted to know even more, and my quest further deepened.

So, on that beautiful fall day in Milwaukee, feeling depressed and unsettled, I went into Barnes & Noble to find comfort, wanting and needing to know more about self-love. I no longer wanted to fill my voids by entering into the wrong relationships. I wanted a beautiful,

loving relationship, to which Anna told me, "If you want a healthy relationship, Karen, you have to be healthy, too." That hit me like a ton of bricks, not in a bad way, but in an eye-opening way. I thought I was healthy? But if I had been healthy, I would have been in a healthy relationship, which clearly, I was not.

From then on, I was determined to become healthy. It became my mission, so I could have a healthy relationship. I know "healthy" doesn't sound as sexy as "passionate," but if you've ever been in a relationship for a long period of time, you know that passion fades and passion doesn't hold your relationship together. It's superficial BS. It's not what makes a relationship work. Healthy individuals make relationships work, and if you ever want a real, long-lasting, loving relationship, you have to strive to be that healthy person and do the inner work. And the benefit of that is passion. Two people who get it. Now, that is sexy.

It was there, in Barnes & Noble. I was searching for a book to help me feel better to quench my thirst to learn more about self-love, that I came across a book called, *Spirit Junkie: A Hip Guide to Happiness* by Gabrielle Bernstein. I remember looking at the front cover and seeing this beautiful blonde-haired woman wearing an aqua-blue sequined tank dress with a big yellow smiley face on it. I remember thinking, "She looks happy. I wonder if she could help make me happy too?" It had been so long since I was happy. I had no idea at the time, but my whole life was about to change.

A year after I purchased Gabby's book, I finally had the courage to make the move back home. Or more accurately, my friend Irene said she was booking a trip to take the ride back with me back home to New York. "Pick a date," she said. Gulp. I picked a date like she said, Friday of Columbus Day weekend. There was no turning back now. The night before I left, I freaked out, just like my life coach said I would. Had she not told me this, who knows. I might have called the whole trip off. I knew I just needed to get over to the other side. Anna, said that once I get back to New York, she was sure I would be fine. The next morning, I waited for my soon to be ex to leave for work and I got my remaining things together. I gave Anabelle the biggest tightest hug ever and said, "good-bye." I got into my over packed car, looked at the house one last time and pulled out of the drive way, and picked up Irene at her hotel nearby before heading out on I-95. On the second night of the drive, Irene was asleep in the passenger seat. It was around 9:00 p.m. when we approached the George Washington Bridge. I could see the New York City skyline in the foreground and tears streamed down my eyes. Fifteen years were behind me; I was finally home.

The next thing I knew, I was at the book launch for Gabby's next book, *May Cause Miracles* at the W Hotel in Union Square. Everything seemed to go into hyperdrive, even though it felt agonizingly slow and painful at the time. To this day, I have no idea how I wound up at Gabby's event, but at the end of the evening, she offered a six-week course on the book. Without hesitation, I signed up for the workshop. The workshop happened to be held at Integral Yoga in Greenwich Village; a block away from the PR firm where I had worked before I got married and moved to the Midwest. I used to pass this studio every day from the subway on my way to work. It was almost as if the Universe was bringing me back to an earlier point to help me make different choices. This was the beginning of Gabby becoming my teacher and mentor. Through Gabby's teachings from the principles of *A Course in Miracles* and her Kundalini yoga training, a whole new perspective of life was opened to me.

I have no doubt that I was guided to find Gabby's book, which led her to be my teacher in New York during my divorce. I know that had I not found this path, my life would have had a completely different outcome. I would have been stuck with the same old mindset—negative, victim-blaming, bitch fest, saying to myself and others, "What can you do? My life sucks." At the same time, I probably would have tried to heal and solve my problems by dating a bunch of guys, trying to find a replacement to fill my now-even-bigger wounds, and winding up in more unhealthy relationships. That would have created a host of other issues. I know for sure that I would not be a life coach, helping others today, and you certainly would not be here reading this book.

~ ~ ~

What I came to realize on this journey was when my ex and I met, he was exactly what I was looking for in a partner (or so I thought). He was smart, handsome, had a great job, honest, wanted kids, came from a good family. And he thought I was what he was looking for in a partner. We had everything society told us we should want to have the American Dream and be happy. We had the house, the careers, dinner dates. Sunday nights we cooked dinner together; he bought me flowers every week. I loved his parents, he loved mine. Even our families loved each other, and yet, we were still so unhappy. That doesn't mean we didn't have good times or that love was gone, but love wears thin with each issue that is never resolved.

We are taught in order to have a happy relationship should have:

✓ Love
✓ Values
✓ Trust
✓ Communication

So what went wrong? Why weren't we happy?

When the marriage ended, I believed it was his fault the marriage failed. I'm usually pretty self-aware, but I honestly could not see my role in what went wrong. I felt I had done everything I believed I could do to save this marriage—leaving positive messages on the bathroom mirror, scheduling us for a couples' marriage retreat, being a loving, supportive wife. I was a good partner, and he even agreed. So, what was my role in it not working out? A friend I had met through a divorce support group in Milwaukee said to me, "Maybe our only fault was that we stayed in it too long." I remember, my first response was, "But I tried everything to make it work?" What I came to understand on my journey was that *you cannot change anyone*. I think for most of our marriage, and in so many other marriages and relationships, we were both trying to change each other into what we wanted the other person to be.

I wanted a "traditional guy." For me, a traditional guy was someone who was loyal, trustworthy and had strong family values. I'm not saying he wasn't; I'm saying this is what I thought in my twenties made a marriage work. That's what I wanted, and that's exactly what the Universe delivered. I will say, in the almost twenty years we were together, he never lied to me. Not once. He was about as honest and trustworthy as they come. Those are very attractive qualities, but on the other side, he was also someone who believed the man should be the head of the household, although he was subtle about it. I wanted a traditional guy, right?

I don't know why it didn't occur to me back then. Probably because he only mentioned it once, and I thought he was kidding. Fine. If he wants a woman who believes he should be the head of the household. I'm sure there is a wonderful woman out there for him, but that just wasn't who I was. I'm someone who believes marriage is a partnership. I guess that was my unspoken requirement. So, there we were, both of us trying to push each other into the roles we assumed for the other. I wanted him to fit in my box of how I thought a partner should be and he wanted me to fit into his. We both should have been more open about it, but I don't think we were aware that was our problem at the time. Most people spend most of their time trying to get their way and trying to be right, and that's what we did, rather than trying to figure out or understand the cause.

No one teaches us how to recognize and choose the right partner. These days many people base their choices on chemistry and passion. If you've wised up, you add values. It's not until we experience pivotal life lessons that we start to learn what works for us and what doesn't. How do you look for something that you don't know you should be looking for? That's why, when we start having real soul-searching, life-changing epiphanies, we are put on these soul-searching quests.

Some of these quests become "awakenings," because before they occur, you are unaware of your need for change. Searching everywhere for the answers, not realizing you were walking around with blinders until you "awaken" and find out—the power was within you all along, you just weren't aware how to access it. Before I experienced my own awakening, I was attracted to articles like, "How to Get the Guy" and "How to Get Over the Guy." Something was missing in between, and it turns out, a lot was missing.

Early on when my husband and I were dating, I didn't have the awareness to realize that our relationship was probably never going to work. I didn't know the early warning signs were there; some I chose not to see. I think many people can relate to that. However, on a spiritual path, everything happens as it should, but awareness helps you see things quicker, which means, if I knew then what I know now, I would have had more clarity in what I wanted and needed in a partner before we married. Intuition may be telling you there are red flags. Having awareness in trusting your intuition is a whole other level.

What I also learned:

1) So many of us were raised to think that once you are in a marriage, you stick it out and make it work. Sometimes to our detriment. I completely support working on our relationships, especially when you are married and made a commitment to that person. Many people give up way too easily when the passion is gone or when it becomes too much work. I worked on a marriage that was never going to work, for twelve years. Somewhere, we have to find the balance between knowing when something is worth fighting for and knowing when it's time to let go. I have no regrets about the time we were together. This is what life is about—learning all these beautiful lessons that help us to learn and grow. I am grateful for his love, support, and friendship that continues to this day.

2) You can't change someone who doesn't want to change, nor do you have the right, just as they have no right to change you. They can only do it for themselves, just as we can only change ourselves. You will save yourself a lot of frustration and heartache once you accept that. We do, however, have a choice:

- To change our perception of the situation
- Accept the situation
- Walk away

We may think we don't have any options when the option isn't what we want. Our egos love blaming the other person and completely avoids taking personal responsibility.

24

However, I've learned that blaming disempowers you, while taking responsibility empowers you. Blame puts the power in their hands. Responsibility puts the power in your hands.

If you do choose to walk away, know that walking away should never be used as a threat. You may have tried this as a tactic in the past to gain control, but it only creates distrust in the relationship. After a while, when your partner realizes you're not leaving, you won't be taken seriously anymore. Only take this option when you know for sure it's time to leave what is not serving your highest good anymore. Once you start understanding that you always have options, you will start using them more wisely.

3) I also came to understand that my ex had every right to want what he wanted in a marriage, just as I did. I wasn't for him, and he wasn't for me. Again, this is awareness. Awareness doesn't look for blame; it knows what is. It allows you to see situations as they really are, rather than how we think they are from our perspective. Once I started putting awareness into practice, I started realizing there is no right or wrong; there just *is*. Awareness helps to relieve the pain and suffering that goes along with blame and puts you in a place of empowerment.

~ ~ ~

Life After Divorce
(Dating Again)

EVEN AFTER MOVING BACK to New York, I stayed in touch with my life coach, Anna. We had phone sessions now instead of office visits. She advised me not to date so soon after the divorce, because I needed time to mourn and process the end of my marriage. I was so blessed to have found Anna, because she was able to tell me what I was going to feel or what might happen, just before it happened. (This shows how unaware I was at the time). When each hurdle came, I knew it was perfectly normal, and I was prepared. Some days, I had Anna on speed dial. But when the final day of the divorce came, a year after I had moved back to New York and two weeks before what would have been our sixteenth wedding anniversary, I felt a part of me was being ripped out from the inside. As if our souls were energetically being ripped apart from one another.

I hated what I was feeling, and I wanted anything to take the pain away. Not listening to Anna's advice, I started dating the seemingly perfect guy. I justified my decision with the fact that it was a few months after the finalized divorce, and four years after the divorce proceedings started. At the time, I thought he was the best boyfriend ever. Well, on the surface.

You know the saying when everything seems too good to be true, it probably is? There was a lot of stuff hiding underneath his well-coiffed, handsome, intelligent, charming, and witty exterior. My relationship with him triggered an old wound in me, reminding me of an old relationship pattern I had before I was married. Once you understand what your

triggers are, you can learn a lot from them when they resurface. If you allow it, they can be healed, but you have to recognize the pattern.

I was able to have a clearer understanding of the intoxicating but sad dance with a charming, emotionally unavailable, covert narcissistic partner. Through this new state of awareness, I was able to remove myself a lot sooner from this relationship, saving myself a lot of heartache and trouble. Had I not done the inner work, I probably would have spent a lot of time trying to salvage the relationship—to bring it back to the way it was, back to when he was the doting, perfect boyfriend who adored me.

I didn't need his love or validation to fulfill me anymore. I had more self-worth through the self-love I was practicing. I was healed and aware enough to recognize that something was off. I was bummed, because it was sad losing someone who enjoyed doing all the same things I did. I believe these are tests from the Universe to see how much we have evolved and learned. I hadn't listened to Anna's advice: I dated too soon for all of the wrong reasons, but this time, I was aware of it, and it was my awareness that pulled me through. I was dating because I didn't want to feel the pain of the ending of my marriage, and I wound up with my next lesson. However, this time, I passed the Universe's test with flying colors.

I will say, at least this guy set the bar high, as a lot of emotionally unavailable partners can do when trying to win the heart of a target. Yes, you read that right: "Target." Emotionally unavailable partners love to get to the juicy part of the relationship, because that's all they want out of the exchange: The fun and excitement and your participation. Doesn't matter if they're not reliable. They don't play by the same rules; it only matters that you're reliable. It also doesn't matter if you're in a relationship with them, live with them, or even married to them. That is why it's so easy for them to leave when things get difficult or replace you with someone new. You're just a playing piece in their game. They're not there to work on anything unless it works to their advantage. That's why nothing seems to improve. They're not in it for you. They're in it for what they can get out of it—the love, fun, and passion—the good times.

At the beginning of the relationship, they'll lavish you with compliments. How much they love and adore you. How they have never met anyone like you before? How different you are from everyone else. Blah, blah, blah. Their only interest is to reel you in. This is why this works so well on people who are desperately seeking love and validation, because they soak this stuff up.

No judgment, I fell for it too. So have millions of others. Male and female. These people know who's susceptible, and they prey on them. It makes them feel they are in control, because their inner world is out of control. They may look like they have their act together on the outside, but on the inside, it's chaos. The truth is they need you more than you need them. This is why it's so important that you do the inner work. It's amazing. After you do the inner work, you start seeing their game a mile away, where you once fell for it. It's as if they are all working from the same playbook, but you're no longer intrigued by them. If anything, it starts feeling like they're desperate or cheesy, and it's a huge turn-off. When you do the inner work, you don't need anyone's love to validate you; you don't need someone telling you you're beautiful. When you do the inner work, you don't want to connect with people in shallow, superficial ways anymore. You have a firm sense of what you want and who you are. You're okay with taking your time. You don't need to be with someone to fulfill you. You are already whole and complete as you are.

I decided to listen to my life coach and take time off from dating, and I also decided to dive deeper into my healing. I studied more, immersing myself in my spiritual practice, learning more about love, life, and myself. And somewhere along the way, I got my certification in life coaching.

~ ~ ~

How This Book
Came to Be

*T*HIS BOOK WAS NOT planned. I was not someone who
ever wanted to write a book. Friends kept telling me to
write a book. But my response was always, "My life and
my story aren't that interesting." However, Gabby's teachings planted a
seed within me. How our stories help to heal other people. I am seeing
this more now as people are waking up, as the wave of the future. It's no
coincidence. It's the Universe working in its mysterious ways. Instead of
hiding our wounds behind closed doors and faking a perfect life publicly,
people are coming out of the darkness and sharing stories of how they
healed to help lift others up and help them heal. This is happening in so
many different communities and industries. I wanted to contribute and
share my healing journey in hopes that others could heal from it too.

After completing my coaching certification, I was working on setting up my platform to become a blogger. The idea of creating a workbook for my coaching clients came to me, but I put it on the back
burner. I wanted to become a blogger first. Then, several people came
forward to me, two acquaintances from my coaching and spiritual
circles told me there was something I was putting off. By the time a
third person shared a similar message, "You know what it is, and you
need to do it now," I didn't need any more messages.

The Universe was trying to get my attention and was telling me to
"Sit down and write this book." Even though I didn't have any experience writing a book, I sat down and started typing what I thought was
going to be a workbook for my clients, not a book. By the time the first

draft was completed, 75,000 words had come through me, and as you know if you read the "Introduction," when it was all said and done, the final book was more than 500 pages and divided into two books: *Healing* and *Moving Forward*. This was a collaborative effort. This work is not all me but was something that came through me through spirit. It certainly was not an overnight process, as I am still learning how to keep the connected flow with the Universe without my ego getting in the way and needing constant distractions. I was happy to hear from established writers that the lure of distractions is part of the creative process.

The lessons and exercises in this book are a culmination of my journey, and the lessons I learned on how to heal from past relationship wounds through the practice of self-love and forgiveness. Lessons that resulted in living a wholeheartedly single life with love and fulfillment. I wrote the book I wish I had read, not before getting married, but before even dating.

If and when you are ready for this process, you will know it. If and when you are ready for the second book on opening your heart again to love, moving forward, and recognizing the right partner, you will know it. This is the start of a practice, you will learn to love and embrace, and I hope you will return, if you need guidance as you navigate your way through this life with resilient love.

What Does it Mean to Heal?

I'VE REFERENCED THE WORD "healing" a few times thus far. If you are new to the practice of healing, from a coaching and spiritual perspective, it means doing the inner work to heal old wounds so they no longer trigger and control us. It's working towards having a new perspective or understanding around something that hurt you. The best is when we have learned from it and become a better person for it, even though you may not completely understand why it happened the way it did. In spite of the pain, you become grateful for the growth you gained.

In coaching and a spiritual journey, we believe we are all born perfect, but over time, our experiences alter our perception of the world. That means you were perfect until the world started distorting and conditioning your perception through unrealistic expectations of perfection, their wounds, and their limiting beliefs. Under all those layers of false perception is still your true form, your soul, which is nothing but pure love without any fear. It is there that you are whole and complete without ego, and its false beliefs hindering us. (We'll get more into how the ego impacts us later in the lessons).

So, what you are "healing" from are all those layers of false, limiting beliefs your ego has formed, beliefs that tell you, "you're not good enough, smart enough, pretty enough, thin enough, or popular enough." Simply put, "you are not worthy enough." Ego seriously brings out the "crazy" in us, or as the Course calls it, "the tiny mad idea." And we cope by attacking other people to protect ourselves when actually we are doing it *to* ourselves. Think of ego as a small,

bratty child that you have to catch in the act and put in the naughty corner. You have to do this so you can receive guidance from your true self, which is your love-based self. Ego is overpowering and demanding and drowns out the voice of our true self. The only way to heal ego is by recognizing it for what it is—your false perceptions. Once you do that, you can reconnect with your true self and the love within you.

If you think about it, everyone can benefit from this practice, because most people live with their ego on automatic pilot. They are unaware of any other way of living. They don't teach it to us in school, so many of us had to discover the truth through our awakening, which showed us how living from ego is not living from the true self. This is why our work here is so important to understand and share, because the world needs so much healing from the ego, especially in our relationships with each other. When we heal and reconnect with our true self, we will minimize personal offense and be less reactive to those we love and even don't love so much. It brings peace to ourselves, our relationships and ultimately, the world. In the next few lessons, you are going to be so grateful, as was I, for this practice, awareness, and freedom.

Dating Detox and
Why it's so Important

HEREVER YOU ARE IN your relationship journey, whether you are dating, not dating or looking to date, I highly recommend that you go on a dating detox while going through the first book of this program. You can start dating again after you have completed this book. Actually, if you are ready to date after you complete this book, it is encouraged you open yourself up to love and start dating again, while living a wholeheartedly single life, which we will cover in Lesson Four. You will have a mindset about dating that is different than the one you had before you began this journey. The purpose of the dating detox is to:

1. Focus purely on yourself, not your "lack of being with someone."
2. Break your addiction and set yourself free from believing you need a partner to complete you.

It's important to note that when you stop dating, it's not to form a shield of independence, but rather, to free yourself from the attachment itself. With a shield of independence you can become content with your life but be closed off to love at the same time to protect yourself. You may find yourself saying, "Yeah, I'm so independent. Who needs anyone?" Instead, what we're aiming for here is someone who is joyful about their life and open to love coming their way, but who doesn't need a date or partner to feel whole, validated, or happy.

If you wear a shield to protect your heart, then you will protect what this program intends to heal. The goal is to open your heart to more love than you could ever imagine. With a dating detox, you will free yourself from the attachment that you need to have someone to complete you. The detox, coupled with the lesson on being whole-heartedly single, teaches you to love your life more, even if you don't have a partner. The loneliness, emptiness, and need will be gone, but you will remain open to meeting a new partner. That's a huge difference.

To make the most of this program, please find where you are in your relationship journey.

A Recent Break Up

If you are experiencing a recent break up, it is more important that you take care of yourself first instead of getting back "in the game" again. You will not find healing in another person, even if it feels like a good distraction. What you will most likely find is frustration and your next mistake, especially if you continue the relationship despite following your intuition and the warning signs. The worst advice is, "In order to get over someone, you have to get under someone." That won't heal you. It just puts a Band-Aid on an open wound to tempo-rarily ease the pain. But later, the same crap is going to keep coming up, because you never properly addressed your wound in the first place. When you keep covering a wound, it only becomes worse over time. Ego has a super good way of rationalizing unhealthy behavior.

There's no denying the trauma of a break-up. The depth of the pain or anger can be so vast that you don't remember what it's like to feel anything else. Especially if it's recent. It can feel so raw. Instead of a date, what you need is emergency self-care and self-love, which are cru-cial right after a break-up. Take the necessary time to be alone and sort things out. Talk to a good friend or a coach. Cry your eyes out, journal, let it all out, and try to understand why things happened the way they did and what your role was in it. Take time to walk in nature or at the beach. You have to give yourself proper time to mourn and heal in order to move on to find the healthy love you want and deserve. Remember, "healthy love" is the love you want, without all of the BS you're so sick of, which is so emotionally draining. Healthy love is real love.

If you do move forward with the dating detox, I can't express how much healing and personal growth you're going to experience. You are a rock star already for choosing to do it! The very purpose of the detox is to release our dependency on other people to save or complete us, which leaves us stronger, more open, independent, emotionally available, more attractive, and able to recognize healthier relationships. Are you ready?

Serial Dater or Serial Monogamist

You really need to get honest with yourself on this one, because you can only help yourself as far as you are willing to go.

- How much do you want real love?
- Are you ready for an emotionally healthy relationship, or are you content with roller coaster relationships that allow you to avoid whatever you are running from, which is usually yourself?
- How committed are you to becoming independent of the need for a partner?

Many serial monogamists have told me they don't know who they are when they come out of a relationship. You need to take time for yourself so you can discover who you really are? You may need to hire a therapist or a coach for deeper discovery into who you really are, but it will be totally worth it. Being on your own may feel uncomfortable at first, but in the end, that discomfort will help you grow and finally be free from co-dependency and your need to have a partner in your life. You will find out more of who you are and what you want, so you don't keep winding up with what you don't want.

I can't force you to do a dating detox, but it is highly recommended that you do it. This is the first step of breaking your co-dependency,

and this program, along with the online community, will be here to support you. If the thought of that frightens you, or you think it's unnecessary to do a dating detox during this program, then it is actually an indicator of your co-dependency. When you're secure in who you are and are content with being alone, the thought of a dating detox won't make you anxious.

If You Haven't Dated in a While

If you haven't dated in a while, this program is designed to help you to heal and release what closed your heart, so you can open your heart to love again. If you haven't dated in a while, you've been on dating detox but not in this way. Switch your focus. That you are not shutting anyone out, but that you are not incomplete without a partner. Somewhere in your subconscious that belief still exists and is holding you back from living your fullest life. You must also be conscious that you are whole and complete without a partner and that your heart is open to love. Even if it's not, just the willingness to open your heart will help to open your heart again to love.

If You Are Currently Dating Someone

No, you do not need to stop dating your current partner to participate in this program. You will still gain a tremendous amount of insight, information, understanding, and healing, which can serve to improve your existing relationship. This program will be a handy tool and resource to go back through, wherever you are in your relationship journey.

~ ~ ~

What Are the Benefits of a Dating Detox?

The goal is to *want* a partner, not *need* a partner. A lot of people say, "Yes, I want a partner! I don't need a partner." Then, ask those same people not to date for six months (which seriously is nothing) and watch them freak out. That's the addiction revealing itself. The ego is really good at justifying our actions, and we even believe it ourselves.

If followed correctly, you will:

✓ Be able to remove your attachment from finding your happiness through someone else.

✓ Be able to be happy and single until you find the right person for you.

✓ Find more fulfillment within yourself and your friendships, since you are not focused on having a partner.

✓ Have less difficulty walking away from partners who are not good for you, since you are no longer dependent on them to make you complete.

✓ Be able to figure out who you are and what you want in a relationship.

✓ Feel more empowered.

✓ Live a wholeheartedly single life.

Yes, I Want Change! I Want to Stay Committed to Myself and to this Program.

What do I Have to do on a Dating Detox?

A dating detox obviously means *no dating*, until you have completed Book One of this program. It also means no dating websites and no texting or flirting with any potential new or ex-lovers, especially those who keep you hooked or occupied, and definitely no hooking up. Period.

Seriously, I've met people who say they're taking a break from dating, but are still hooking up with their ex. That's like saying you're on a diet but eating stale cupcakes on the side. It's an emotional crutch and it doesn't work when you're trying to remove your addiction and attachment to love.

It's a commitment to you and the love you have for yourself. You are breaking the need to have someone in your life to fill any voids to cover past wounds. You can't heal those wounds if you keep covering them with distractions. You have to uncover and feel the discomfort that comes with loneliness in order to heal and be free. You'll be so busy taking care of you, you won't have time to feel lonely.

Are you committed to yourself and your healing and freedom?

Sign here: _____

Date: _____

Resilient Love

*R*ESILIENT *LOVE* is a self-study course, so go at your own pace; however, it is suggested to try to do one lesson per week to get into a practice. But go with what makes you most comfortable. The most important thing is that you get the most out of each lesson, and you develop a practice.

For most of the lessons there will be:

- An affirmation related to the lesson.
- Guidance for your meditation and intention practice.
- Journal exercises—It is encouraged that you write out the journal exercises. However, if you are not a writer (and some of us are not), you may reflect and meditate on the questions and the lesson throughout the day, which is better than not doing the exercises or this program at all.

    Writing helps to get out everything that you have been holding in and sometimes see it from a different perspective. Writing can have the same releasing effect as talking to a good friend.

~ ~ ~

Supplies

Items you will need for this course:

- **A journal**—For your writing exercises or dive deeper writing about your thoughts and epiphanies after each lesson.

- **Colorful note paper**—You will use the paper to jot down affirmations or write words to keep in your pocket as a reminder.

- **An altar (optional)**—You can create a beautiful altar. The altar is a place where you honor yourself, your commitment, your intentions, and your connection with God, the Universe, angels, or whatever makes you feel most connected to the light within you. Rituals help to keep you committed and are a beautiful part of the practice. The altar can include a candle you light when you say a prayer, set an intention, or meditate. You can also place items, beautiful words, affirmations, prayers, poems, flowers, anything you wish on your altar. It is your sacred space to honor yourself, give thanks, and connect to the divine within you. At your altar, you will be setting intentions each day on the lesson for that week. Share photos of your altar with the Resilient Love Book Club Facebook group.

Your Personal Growth Toolkit
Quick Reference Guide

*A*LONG WITH THE EXERCISES in this book, you can use all kinds of tools, from meditations to practicing affirmations, to help you stay aligned with what you want. When you're stressed, you can meditate. If you're freaking out about something, which freaking out seldom ever serves us well, then "releasing" or "letting go" by walking, running, and surrendering on your yoga mat are useful tools to help you feel more centered. Then, you can use journaling or meditatation to help you understand and release more. This is where you can get creative. Use whichever tools work best for you.

Tools are extremely helpful when you know how to use them. One of the most important things about using tools is knowing what works best for you, what tools to use and when, and knowing how to balance your tools. Everything in life is like a balance scale. If we add too much forgiveness, we become a doormat. If we add too much protection, we become hard. If we add too much non-attachment, we become void. If we become too attached, we go crazy. If we try to control too much, we lose control. The key is to always find your balance.

Affirmations

Affirmations are a wonderful tool to help you get motivated and stay aligned. However, it's important to mention, if you're having a meltdown and really triggered by something, throwing an affirmation on top of something that's really upsetting you is not going to be effective. You need something stronger to release it first. Yoga, journaling,

and even running are much more effective tools when you are having a difficult time. However, affirmations are extremely useful tools for managing negative thoughts before they take over or switching old, negative thinking patterns into healthy thought patterns. Affirmations are perfect if you are having self-doubts or judging yourself too harshly.

Sample affirmation: *"I am whole and complete within myself. I love and accept myself exactly as I am."*

Notice if you feel shift in your body and mindset? How it makes you feel? That's how you know an affirmation is working.

Dance!

Dancing is a wonderful way to shift your energy. Turn up the music out loud or on your headphones and dance by yourself. Dancing is great for releasing minor annoyances that are only dragging you down, and it helps to increase your level of joy. What song do you have to dance to whenever you hear it? Turn it up!

Non-Attachment

This is a wonderful tool to use if you suffer from anxiety, take things too personally, and focus too much on everything that is going on around you. It helps you to be less reactive in situations by not embracing false perceptions. Non-Attachment should not be confused with indifference, becoming emotionally numb, escaping, or running away from something emotional. It's important to use these tools properly. Non-Attachment is used so we do not allow our emotions to control us and drive us further into fear, anger, or worry. Non-Attachment is best used to stop overthinking through reframing and understanding your triggers.

Meditation

Meditation is used to help you center and bring you back to your calm, rational state of mind. The point of meditation is not relaxation although that is a benefit. The point of meditation is to calm the mind to have more clarity, awareness and connection to your true self and to Spirit. Meditation has been scientifically proven to shrink the amygdala, which is responsible for emotions such as fear, anger, sadness, and aggression. The larger our amygdala, the more reactive we will be and more likely to act from our fears with anger or aggression. Meditation increases the left hippocampus in our brain, which is responsible for our self-aware-ness and empathy. Meditation does not control your thoughts but keeps them from controlling you.

Mindfulness

Mindfulness is the practice of being aware in the present moment. Ancient philosopher Lao Tzu accurately described mindfulness by stating, "When you are depressed, you are living in the past. When you are anxious, you are living in the future." Mindfulness helps you stay in the here and now. A mindfulness practice of paying attention to your thoughts and emotions and whether you are responding vs. reacting to them. It means observing what is happening without judg-ment. A mindfulness practice also includes loving kindness, compas-sion, and acceptance of yourself and others.

Music

Play a song that complements your practice for the week's lesson to help keep you aligned with what you want to release or bring in. Music, like dance, can be used to increase your energy. It can also be used as a tool to help you center and relax.

Reframing

Reframing takes negative thoughts that aren't serving you and changes them into thoughts that do work for you. When you reframe and find a new belief that resonates and works for you, you feel a shift in your mind and energy. Every moment you have an opportunity to choose a loving thought over a negative one.

Example of a Negative Thought:
"I've tried everything. Nothing works for me."

Example of a Loving Thought:
"It may take time, but I know I'll find a way."

Surrender

Surrendering is one of the best tools for releasing. Surrender, in this world is defined as giving up. However, surrendering in the spiritual world is asking the Universe to release something from you, help you interpret it differently, or guide you in the situation. One of the best places to surrender is on a yoga mat in child's pose. If you're not familiar with child's pose, you get down on your knees with your body and arms extended out in front of you on the floor. From this position, you are literally asking God, "Please take this from me. Please help me to see it another way." Repeat as often as necessary.

Yoga

Just like meditation, yoga is another excellent practice to center the mind. Yoga is the active practice for meditation.

Walking in Nature

Walking in nature is another way to release negative energy, increase endorphins, and connect with yourself. Try a walking meditation, where you clear your mind of any outside distractions, including not using any headphones. Just take in the fresh air and be mindful of the beautiful energy of nature that's around you. Notice the trees, the earth and sky. Similar to yoga, you are exercising your body along with your mind.

~ ~ ~

A Word About Resistance

ESISTANCE MAY BE SOMETHING you experience throughout this process. We all have resistance.

Remember your ego is like a bratty child. There are times when that inner child will simply not want to do something, or more likely, not want to see or admit something. Resistance can be at a conscious or subconscious level. If you are aware that there is something you definitely don't want to face, then take your time and come back to it when you are ready. However, you cannot release what you are not ready to face or recognize. There's a difference between something that you reject out of resistance and something you reject because it's not aligned with your truth.

Resistance feels more like you are pushing something away. Like, "Nah, I don't need that," when it's exactly what you need. It may sound like, "This is a load of bull," or "That's just not vibing with me." That's definitely resistance with ego talking. When something is not aligned with your truth, it resonates deep within your soul. It feels more like, "I should not do that." It's a, "Hell no!" There could be a lot fear with resistance, too. Fear can resonate in the thoughts that say, "I'm afraid" or "I'm not ready;" however, something not aligned with your soul says, "I should not go down that path. This feels wrong." After you face your resistance, you should feel free and empowered as you step into it, because you are releasing so many fears, which is why people stay on this path—for the freedom.

Your ego resists, because it's trying to protect its survival. Ego will erect walls, be defensive, and keep you separate from love and your spiritual connection. Ego likes to think it's practical, but practicality fears risk and keeps you stuck. Practicality, in essence, is a killer of dreams. People who succeed take a lot of risks and try new things to see what works. Successful people don't think in terms of, "What if it doesn't work?" They think, "Let's see how I can make it work!" Ego thinks power is contained by building walls to keep you safe, when the exact opposite is true. Real power is expansive and without limitations.

Please keep an open mind during this process of de-layering. We only understand messages at the level of awareness we are ready to receive; the more open and willing you are to the process, the more you will receive. So, be patient and do not judge yourself. Always accept where you are in the process. You are never too late. You are always right where you are supposed to be.

However, based on your level of awareness, it is up to you to recognize and understand if your ego is facing any resistance and why. Only you can do this work. There is no cheating or manipulating the Universe or your Universal lessons. No one can do the work for you. How you show up and how much you show up will reflect in your progress. You must understand, this journey is about practice, never perfection. It's building a healthy foundation and strengthening your awareness muscles.

The steps at the beginning of this journey are:

- Keep an open mind.
- Be patient with yourself.
- Accept where you are.
- Be proud of yourself for doing this work.

We are now ready to proceed onto Lesson One.

~ ~ ~

Childhood Wounds

(Optional or You Can Come Back To This
Later and Move onto Lesson Two)

*Painful lessons I learned about love as a child,
I came to understand was not love,
and do not define me*

How We Learn What Love Is?

Originally, this lesson on childhood wounds was not in the book. It came about while I was beta testing this program. A couple of the participants had a similar issue while reading the original first lesson on forgiveness. Most of the wounds that came up when they were looking for someone who they needed to forgive stemmed from their relationship with their parents, or one particular parent, during their childhood.

I had moved past my own healing with my relationship with my father long before I became a transformational coach; however, my relationship with him had everything to do with the partners I chose. All our relationships and how we view love stems from our relationships with our parents and their relationship with each other, as well as what we witnessed as "love" during our childhood. I know some of you who are reading this may not have lived with your birth parents, but with a relative, perhaps a grandparent, an aunt, a family friend, foster or adoptive parents.

Your childhood experience with love sets your foundation for love. Growing up, was your experience with love abundant or scarce? Did you feel loved or not loved as a child? It doesn't matter if it was a biological parent, what matters is how you bonded? How we bonded

with our parents or guardian affects how we bond with our partners today. It's how our attachment styles are formed. Whether you have a secure attachment style or insecure attachment with a partner is based on those early childhood connections. How you developed your ability to bond or not bond, is not your fault, but our healing is our responsibility.

We all come into this Earth wanting to be loved. If we didn't get that love or form a bond with our parent or guardian, we may have developed an insecure attachment style, which is when someone wants to get close to you, but you pull away and sometimes run away. This is your ego trying to protect you from getting hurt again. Although you may long for connection, it feels unfamiliar and unsafe to you. Someone with a healthy bond with their parent or guardian most likely has a secure attachment style. They feel safe in a close relationship with their partners.

People with an insecure attachment style will often be drawn to partners who reject them or whose love they must earn, recreating the same insecure attachment they had with that parent. Nevertheless, once they win the partner over, they sometimes surprisingly lose interest in that partner, but if their partner also has an insecure attachment style, the two wind up in a push-and-pull dance, which is when your partner gets too close, and you pull away. Then when your partner pulls away, you try to get close. It's a vicious cycle. Subconsciously, both believe they are unworthy of love or fear they will lose that love, so to protect themselves, they reject it first before it can hurt them. Remember, ego believes it is protecting you and keeping you safe, even though it is hindering you from fully loving and being loved. Your goal is to recognize and manage your ego, so you can create the love you do want in your life, rather than having it control you into further loveless despair.

After the feedback from my beta testers, I knew I had to go back and rewrite this workbook to start with a lesson on *The Childhood Wound*. If participants in my beta testing group were dealing with these emotions, and I know what a huge role this wound played in my life, it would be the same for so many of you reading this book. I do not claim to be an expert on childhood wounds (also known as the Parent Wound), but I have done a great deal of research. Through my own experience as a life coach, I want to help you to start exploring this area, so you can become aware of what is holding you back and finally be free of it, or at least, aware of it, so you can get closer to having the relationship you desire.

Even though your childhood wounds may have been brought to light, your journey towards healing those wounds may not end here. You might want to explore this further with a therapist or life coach who specializes in it.

The goal is not to blame our parents or guardians for our current condition. As children we expected them to be perfect, but as you grow older, you come to realize that they are wounded imperfect human beings, just as we are. The way they cared for us stems from how they were raised by their parents or guardians, and how those parents and guardians were raised, and so on. The purpose of examining your childhood wounds is to build an awareness around how your relationships with them influenced your perception and foundational knowledge of love.

Do you have to be completely healed from all of your childhood wounds to enter a relationship? Absolutely not. If that were true, none of us would be in a relationship. No one on this earth is completely healed of all their love wounds. We all carry varying levels of wounds from our childhoods and past relationships. But it will help you to understand your triggers, so you can witness and address them, rather than act upon them. This lesson is the start of your healing journey.

~ ~ ~

We are all born a blank slate—pure, innocent, perfect. All we want when we arrive on Earth, is to love and be loved. However, over time, our experiences with love shaped our perception of what love actually means. To many, love means hurt and pain. That is a skewed perception. There is no double meaning of love. Love simply means *love*. Love feels full, abundant, safe, and secure. It never feels like lack, unworthiness, or mistrust. Anything that does not feel like love is not love.

Everyone is influenced by the way their parents or guardians loved them, whether we considered it good or bad. It should be noted, that there necessarily is no "right" or "wrong," but whether or how much we are either moving towards love or away from love into fear. Our

work is to be aware of the direction we are moving in. The more we try to understand, the more we expand our awareness to view a situation from all sides—our perspective, their perspective, and seeking the truth from our higher intuitive self. We are better at assessing what really happened rather than assessing a situation from ego's perception, also known as "constricted awareness." If we are not thinking from all sides, we are most likely thinking from ego's perspective. Viewing a situation from all perspectives brings greater understanding. When you understand why a situation happened and why a lesson was brought to you, personal evolution and growth occurs.

Some of us on this Earth had positive experiences with our parents. However, even the most well-meaning parents can have dysfunctional or harmful effects on a child, sometimes without the child even realizing. For example, a parent who is too strict may believe that is how to help a child succeed, without considering the psychological pressure they put on the child. Sometimes well-meaning parents may coddle their children too much and do everything they can for them, which results in helpless and self-centered children. They grow up and don't understand why the world doesn't do everything for them the way their parents did. It is not your partner's role to take care of you the way your parents did, and you may be unaware and blame your partner for this. A real, non-codependent relationship is when two whole people work in partnership together. Narcissistic children are raised by parents who either loved and praised them too much or didn't love them enough. For the latter, the need for love is so great, they need to be in control of it to feel secure.

Our parents' perception of love, their ability to express love, and how much they love themselves greatly influenced how we felt loved and how we view love and relationships. It also set the tone for how worthy we feel of love. If you had a parent who was very generous with love, you may feel worthy of receiving love. However, if you grew up with a parent who had a difficult time expressing love, you may not feel worthy of being loved. You may also feel that love is something you have to work for and earn, because that was the only time you received positive attention from your parent. Instead of receiving unconditional love, your parents' affection was based on conditions and performance.

Your childhood wounds greatly impacts who you select as a partner, whether you realize it or not. The childhood wound is your core wound. If the wound is deep, it will keep showing up in every relationship until you become aware of it and heal it. If you want the love you say you want, then it's in your best interest, and yours alone, to heal it as best you can. If your mother or father withheld love, you may believe that love involves the pain associated with needing and longing for love from a person who is unequipped to give it. This is not what love is. The more unloved you felt as a child, the more likely you will choose partners whose love you have to earn to prove you are worthy of love. At the same time, you will be turned off by healthy partners whose love you don't have to win, or you will sabotage any chances at real love because you don't trust love and subconsciously you don't believe anyone could love you or that you are worthy of love, because no one taught or showed you that you were worthy of love. Your childhood environment conditioned your brain's definition of love, and you may be forever chasing elusive love. Love always seems just out of reach for you.

Your wounds can only affect you as much as you allow them. If you believe you have trust issues and are the victim of abandonment, then you will perceive the world as an unsafe place filled with people who will betray or abandon you. By keeping this mindset, your beliefs will create self-fulling prophecies. This is when you subconsciously create a life that matches your beliefs.

You may be worried that someone is going to cheat on you. Because of this, you don't give anyone you're dating a chance. You question your partner's whereabouts, or frequently check up on them to ensure they are not lying to you. Subconsciously, you will either attract someone who will confirm your beliefs and hurt you, or you will be a wreck, so worried they might be cheating on you, even if they aren't. Your fear-based thinking and energy are literally shifting the dynamic of the relationship from a loved-based connection to a fear-based connection, causing unnecessary stress in the relationship. Or, you may be the one to cheat on your partner, to protect yourself from getting too attached to one person. Maybe you're afraid of getting hurt, and you may keep your distance in the relationship to avoid getting too close, for fear of getting hurt again, steering away from any real intimacy or bonding activities. Everything in the relationship will

be at a surface level to protect your heart. You might fear your partner may abandon you, and you may become controlling to the point they leave; thus, fulfilling your self-fulfilling prophecy of abandonment. You just proved yourself right, but instead of understanding that you created the outcome due to your actions towards them, you blame them for leaving you and default back to your limiting, fearful beliefs about being unlovable and unworthy. We all have relationship fears, it depends on how aware you are of them and how you choose to respond, rather than react from, your wound.

A better approach is to be aware of your wounds and triggers. You can reframe these beliefs by saying, "I am not what happened to me. I am healing and creating awareness around my triggers, so they no longer control my life. I can create a happier, healthier, better life, one that I always dreamed of, with this partner." If you believe you may have a deep childhood wounds due to a narcissistic, borderline, depressed, absent, bipolar, or alcoholic parent, you can certainly continue with this program. You will find benefit from it, but I strongly suggest you explore deeper into this with a therapist, books, or programs on healing that particular type of childhood wound. The exercises below will help you get started.

There are so many books and workshops, and even online support groups, in this area. If you decide to continue exploring this further, my only suggestion is that you seek a program that is loved based. The program should not blame the parent, but help create awareness and understanding for true healing to occur. Blame never heals. It may help you feel validated, understood, and even empowered, which are all important aspects of the healing process, but blame most likely will create more walls, resentment, and judgement. As difficult as this may seem right now, true healing requires letting go of what hurt you and redefining it in another way, because it breaks down walls that will ultimately set you free. You won't need to build a fort to protect yourself, because you will learn how to set healthy boundaries and trust yourself.

As you continue onto the exercises, please remember this...

You are not your past, what happened to you or your wound.
You are the hope for healing and light that shines within you.

Exercises to Help Create Awareness Around Your Childhood Wound

The following exercises are designed to help you create awareness around childhood wounds, so you can begin the healing process. Healing can take time and come gradually. You may want to come back to this exercise after you complete the book to see how your answers have changed.

These questions will not be triggering for most of you but if you feel very strong emotions arise, please contact a therapist or call 911 for immediate support.

Day 1: Journal or Self-Observation

During these exercises, you can choose to journal or observe your thoughts. It's more effective if you journal but thinking them over is better than not doing these exercises at all or not moving forward. Don't let journaling keep you from doing these exercises.

Journal or observe your thoughts to raise your awareness around your earliest experiences about love. Answer as many questions as you feel comfortable answering.

Questions:

- What was love like in your household? Was it expressed or not expressed openly?
- What did love mean to your mother, father, or guardian?
- Were your parents or guardians affectionate with each other?
- Did you feel they loved one another?
- Were your parents or guardian affectionate with you?
- Did your parents or guardian favor one child over another?
- What was your relationship like with your mother, father, or guardian?
- Did you feel loved?

Write out all your answers and feelings associated with those questions.

Meditation

Light the candle and sit in meditation. If you feel emotional after the exercise, set an intention by asking God, the Universe, or your higher self to help you surrender and release these heavy emotions that have been holding you down for so long. Trust that it will be released from you. And know that you are loved and supported.

One of my favorite yoga positions for surrender and release as I mentioned earlier is child's pose. Child's pose where you kneel with your torso and arms laid out on the ground in front of you, as if you are bowing deeply before God and the Universe and asking them to take what you are feeling from you and help you to interpret it a new way with understanding. Feel the Universe's love and compassion for you as it helps you to release it. You may need to surrender and release a lot in the beginning, if emotions are very strong. Repeat as often as necessary. If writing is cathartic, focus on the feeling of the release and letting go. Take any notes on what comes up for you.

You can sit in silence and focus on today's lesson and set your intentions for your meditation, or visit my website for your free bonus meditation on "Healing Childhood Wounds" at:

karenOM.com/resilient-love-meditations
Password: resilientlover

You are also free to use one of the many meditations on YouTube. Healing is about whatever works best for you. It's not the same for everybody, but the goal is to release your emotions in a healthy way. The recommended amount of time to sit in meditation is at least 20 minutes. You can choose to close your eyes during meditation or focus gently on a candle. If you are new to this, you can start with as little as 5 to 7 minutes. Meditation is highly recommended, a life-changing part of this practice, so please do not skip this.

Give it a chance.

Intention

An intention is something you want to bring in. It could be something like:

- "Help me to release this."
- "Please help me to understand this."
- "Please help me to forgive."

For this exercise, your intention could be: "Please help to release this hurt, pain, and anger from me." Or you can write your own intention. Always follow what your intuition and what your soul is telling you at any point during this program.

Day 2

Exercise: Journal or Self-Observation

Journal or observe your thoughts. Today, start writing to build your awareness around your relationship with your parents.

The question to have in mind: *How did your relationship with your parents or their relationship with each other affect your views on love and how you view yourself today?*

Leave two pages blank to come back to later.

Meditate

Sit in silence and set your intentions for 5 to 20 minutes, while you focus on the awareness you created around today's lesson and exercise, or use the meditation again on "Healing Childhood Wounds" from my website. This is your practice, do what you feel is best for you.

Day 3

Exercise: Journal or Self-Observation

Journal or observe your thoughts. Start building your awareness around how your perceptions of love influenced your romantic relationships.

Questions:

✓ How have your wounds or your views on love been influencing your choices of partners?

✓ How has this wound affected how you connected, or didn't connect, with your partners?

✓ What are some other ways this wound has been showing up in your relationships?

Know that you are not your wounds. You are bringing awareness to witness the wound so you can heal it.

Leave the next two pages blank to come back to later.

Meditate

Set your intentions and sit in silence for anywhere from 5 to 20 minutes, focusing on your intention and the awareness you created around today's exercise.

You are doing awesome. Keep going.

Day 4
Exercise: Journal or Self-Observation

Journal or observe your thoughts. Today, try to start seeing your parent for who they are, not who you want them to be. (Only answer questions that apply to your situation).

Questions:

✓ We don't know everything about our parents or guardians, but given what you do know who or what made them who they were when they raised you?

✓ Do you feel they did the best they could from their level of awareness?

✓ See your parents like you—as a wounded child. To help give you a better understanding of the dynamic you had with them, consider: What was their childhood like?

✓ Did your parents come from healthy childhood homes? Can you see how any fear-based thoughts created the world they live in?

✓ If your parent is an alcoholic or suffers from a mental illness, are you willing to start taking steps toward accepting their limitations? What steps can you take to understand their circumstance better? Understanding does not mean what they did was okay, but that you understand what made them the way they are.

✓ How have some of your parents' limiting or fear-based beliefs affected you? What can you do to change those beliefs, so you don't repeat the cycle? How can you reframe those limiting or fear-based beliefs to empower you through love?

Ask God or your higher self for guidance to help you see it differently. Choose to see your parents and/or guardian with love over fear.

Meditate

Set your intentions and sit in silence, focusing on the awareness you created around today's lesson and exercise anywhere for around 5 to 20 minutes, or use my free meditation on "Healing Childhood Wounds" on my website, listed under "Meditation" under the first exercise.

Day 5 Exercise: Review Previous Journals

Today, go back to your notes from Days 2 and 3, if you journaled.

✓ Are you willing to see your patterns that are not serving you well?

✓ Are you willing to see all sides of the story with love, whether it's love for your parents (knowing they were trying to do the best they could from their level of awareness), love for yourself, or both?

✓ Are you willing and ready to identify your false beliefs about love and the stories that were created behind them?

✓ Even if what happened was real, can you recognize any fear-based beliefs that are holding you back today? For instance, having a mother who could not love you the way you needed to be loved, knowing that it does not mean that you are unlovable. Her inability to love you is not the truth; the truth is you are loveable. Perhaps you had a father who wasn't present. His not being present had nothing to do with you not being loveable either. Why was he not present? Was he working hard to provide for the family? Did he have his own wounds that made him feel unworthy as a father? Did he grow up in an era where he believed that parenting was the mother's role?

It is said we cannot see someone's truth unless we see them through our highest self. What is your heart, your highest self, telling you about these stories and beliefs? What growth and understanding can be found from this introspection?

Meditate

Set your intention and sit in silence, focusing around the awareness you created today, for anywhere from 5 to 20 minutes.

Day 6 Exercise: Beginning the Practice of Forgiveness

Note: If you are having a difficult time with the word "forgiveness," please replace it with "let go" or "letting go."

Today's exercise will start the practice of forgiveness. I understand this exercise may be hard for some of you. To those who've had very difficult childhoods that seem unforgiveable, honor and respect where you are. You are not left behind. Feel free to move on to the next lesson on Forgiveness to gain more awareness on what it can do for you, and how and why forgiving or letting go, is one of the best practices to set yourself free from the past.

Forgiveness is not something you can simply jump into, even if you want it. Forgiveness or letting go, is a practice, another awareness muscle that you build.

For those ready to forgive or at least give it a chance, write in your journal any revelations you may have had during the last exercise on seeing through the lens of love and how you may forgive your parents or guardians for any childhood wounds you have today understanding that they were doing the best they could from their level of awareness. How did their limitations make you a better person today? Sometimes people show us who we don't want to be? Try seeing through the lens of love and compassion helps us to open our hearts. Understanding the wounds helps us to heal the pattern.

You do not need to forgive them in person. You are forgiving the wound within you, and you are forgiving them at an energetic level, releasing yourself from any ties to the negativity that have been holding you back. You may have heard that forgiveness is not "for them," but for you, to set yourself free and move forward. It's not about what they have done, but about the fact that you are no longer allowing their actions to control you or affect you.

You may also want to forgive yourself in this exercise, especially if you are experiencing guilt about your feelings towards your parents or caretakers. Many people who do these forgiveness exercises feel a shift in their relationship with the person they forgive. Sometimes the person even calls or messages them.

The purpose of this exercise is to allow necessary emotions to surface, so they can be understood, released, and healed. If you feel stuck, ask for guidance from God or your highest self on how to heal this situation, offering it to the highest good for everyone involved.

Meditate

Set your intentions and sit in silence, focusing on the awareness you created today, from 5 to 20 minutes.

Day 7 Exercise: Reflection

Today, focus on what you have released and uncovered.

Questions:

✔ What awareness has it raised for you about your wounds and triggers in relationships?

✔ What further steps can you take to build stronger, healthier, and more intimate relationships?

Meditate

To deepen your practice, light a candle and set your intentions, then meditate anywhere from 5 to 20 minutes, focusing on the awareness you created today. You can also choose to use one of your favorite meditations from YouTube.

Forgiveness, Letting Go, Non-Attachment, Acceptance

Forgiveness is
the greatest gift you can give yourself

Note: If you are having a difficult time with the word "forgiveness," please replace it with "let go" or "letting go."

Why Should I Forgive Someone Who Hurt Me?

You may already be familiar with the concept of forgiveness as part of an emotional-spiritual healing practice, since we covered a bit of it in the last lesson. But for those of you who are not, it is essential that you keep an open mind throughout this lesson. At first, it may be a difficult concept to embrace, so go at your own pace and always accept where you are. I promise, if you can get to a place of forgiveness, you will finally find freedom and peace in your heart you've always wanted. Not recognizing the importance of forgiveness, and staying in unforgiveness, you will continue to store the pain in your heart rather than being free of it. A strong practice in unforgiveness may feel empowering, but it only serves to negatively impact you and all your relationships, whether you realize it or not.

Forgiveness may not feel as empowering as not forgiving someone, but it is one of the most effective healing tools available. We should really call them "freedom tools," because that's what healing does; it gives you freedom. It releases you from the harm they caused you. However, most of society relies on their egos to guide

them through their difficult and emotional challenges. Relying on ego's coping mechanism is like allowing an angry, unsupervised child to manage your emotions. Ego's shallow awareness will lead you to believe that unforgiveness is empowerment and forgiveness lets the offender off the hook and is a sign of weakness. However, holding onto that anger and bitterness can wreck your life. If you're letting someone else's action have that kind of control over you and your life because you still feel bitter about being victimized over it, that's not very empowering is it?

You're not punishing them; you're punishing yourself. An unwillingness to forgive directly blocks you from moving forward in your life. The best revenge is no revenge at all. Your best revenge is saying, "I moved on, learned from it, and created a better life for myself."

Of course, embracing forgiveness doesn't mean we should dismiss what we are feeling. We are human, after all, and we are going to have emotions, because they are a natural part of our lives. Our emotions are important guides. While joy and love are preferable emotional states, sadness and anger reveal what is important to us, what we value, and where we may need to set boundaries. Most importantly, triggers can help us identify where we still need healing.

Suppressing emotions often leads to depression and numbing addictions, such as alcohol, sex, and drug abuse—anything to run away from the pain. The healthier option is to learn how to understand, manage, and balance our emotions.

Love puts us in a very vulnerable state, and if we are hurt by someone we love—hurt, pain, and anger will inevitably follow. These emotions take a toll on our bodies, and can cause stress, hypertension, and heart disease. This is why it is important to release negative energy and pent-up emotions from our bodies, before they have time to accumulate and cause long-term damage. In fact, scientific studies have revealed that the chemical compound of tears contains toxins, and the physical act of crying releases endorphins, which is why we feel so much better after a good cry.

During this lesson, I encourage you to cry your eyes out and release those toxins and build up those endorphins in your body. Cry, scream, punch a pillow—whatever works. Accept what you are feeling and repeat as often as necessary. The important part is to just get it out and know that your own inner guidance brought you here, because it knew it was time to let this go and finally heal.

As you start building your awareness around the power of forgiveness, you will start to realize how much control you have over the situation, as opposed to the situation being in control of you. It's an incredibly empowering position to be in, one that your ego is not aware of, but your higher self is. Each piece of the past you leave behind gives you permission to live a freer, happier life.

The best and most surprising benefit of forgiveness is that it sets you free from your own self-imposed prison. Our ego desperately wants us to hold onto anger, because it thinks it's protecting us while punishing the other person. But being stuck in anger and resentment doesn't do anything to the other person. It only hurts us, and to our chagrin, the more we are stuck in unforgiveness and anger, the less empathetic the person who hurt us seems towards us. Ever notice how that happens? In every situation, there are two sides to every story, but when we are hurt, we usually only see our side. *A Course in Miracles* teaches that any grievance we have against another person is an illusion, what we think we see is something that is actually not there, but based on something that happened to us in the past. When we refuse to see another person's side, it blinds us from the truth. The Course also asks, "Would you rather be right or happy?" Ego thinks being right makes us happy, but once you become aware of this, you will begin to realize you can't have both. Always having to be right, prevents us from being happy, and doesn't make us very enjoyable to be around.

Maybe you have tried to understand their side of the story, but you're still upset because they're not taking any responsibility. It may help you to understand if your grievance is with someone who suffered some type of abuse as a child. Many adults who suffered from abuse as children remain emotionally at the age when the trauma occurred, unless they have been through counseling or have healed spiritually from those wounds. Studies have shown that children who have suffered from child abuse or neglect have brains that have developed differently when compared to those who did not experience abuse as children. It doesn't matter how successful or educated someone is; if they have not addressed those wounds, they will most

likely regress to the age and act out of that wound during a disagreement or stress in the relationship. They will use the tactics they have learned over the years designed to protect them when they are triggered. They are in survival mode.

We all have experienced some type of trauma in our lives, and we all do this to some extent, but adults who were abused as children may be unable to take responsibility for their behavior, because it is associated with their childhood wound. They have difficulty separating their actions from their identity. This is especially true if they are perfectionists; they work so hard at being "perfect" with everything they do. Every decision is made with precision; they cannot be wrong. Wrong means being bad or not good enough. Possibly rejection or punishment from a parent. The moment you address them about something, their ego is so quick to justify their actions and project the blame onto you. It may make you feel like you are going crazy, but you are not going crazy. This is their ego's self-defense mechanism to protect the small child within. It may not make any sense to you, and they may not even realize they are doing it, as it takes a certain level of self-awareness to recognize the many nuances of our own behavior.

Forgiveness requires us to take a step back and put ourselves in another person's shoes, trying to see things as they really are. As we did in the exercise in the last lesson, "The Childhood Wound." While we can understand and be compassionate towards someone's wounds, it doesn't mean we have to tolerate behavior that is disrespectful of us. This is where learning to set healthy boundaries is required. Also, as responsible evolving adults, we must see how we may have contributed to an undesired outcome as well.

Shifting perspective is definitely not easy when it comes to some situations that need forgiving. Viewing the situation from the other person's perspective in no way lets them off the hook, but it helps to create a deeper understanding of the situation as a whole, since most of the time we are entirely focused on our side of the story. Shifting perspective doesn't mean you agree, but that you are perceiving the situation from a higher perspective of wisdom. Ask yourself:

- What can I learn here?
- How does this experience help me to grow?

- How can I use this situation to make better decisions and create better outcomes in the future?

Someone may have done something beyond hurtful to you, but keeping that pain alive is only giving them power to break your heart over and over again. Your wounds cannot heal if you keep reinjuring them. They may have hurt you once or many times, but you continue to hurt yourself by revisiting that pain over and over again. It's almost like building a shrine to the person who hurt you and worshipping them with that pain every day. If someone hurt you, they don't deserve for you to honor them every day with your pain. Moving on and letting it go helps you to live a happier life. This is why wisdom says, "Forgiveness isn't for them; it's for you."

It can be extremely hard to understand the concept of forgiveness. Even if you do understand it and are willing to forgive, it can still be hard to forgive. You may be in the thick of intense emotions right now and can't forgive. Just accept where you are. I teach this, I can still have a hard time forgiving someone when it's too soon. That's when something has triggered a deep wound and ego has tight grip on us (to protect us), and we can't see past the filter it has placed before our eyes. It can shift our entire perception of a situation from one moment to the next, especially after a breakup where anger and hurt are involved, and it's still so raw. We hit those highs and lows. The only difference for me now is, I know beyond ego's illusion how much peace, happiness, and freedom are on the other side of forgiveness.

It also made me realize how much control I have over my own suffering through the power of forgiveness. Forgiveness brings inner peace, and I know now, there is nothing or no one worth giving up that peace of mind. Now, I feel so much more empowered when I align myself with forgiveness, because whoever hurt me and whatever happened no longer has any control over me.

When you can reinterpret it and create a new level of awareness around it, that is the miracle in a shift in perception. That is the gift you get out of it, the gift that propels you to a higher level of consciousness. Higher thinking allows us to move forward and create a new story that works for us, rather than against us.

Keep in mind, you cannot force yourself to forgive someone. There are people who you may want to forgive but still can't. There's no faking this. Your heart is always aware when something doesn't feel authentic, but all you need is a willingness to want to forgive and it begins opening the channels. Give yourself time and ask the Universe to help you reinterpret this for healing in your heart. It's easier to forgive when you have a clearer understanding of why you are forgiving. If you are still having difficulty, don't worry, you are not doing anything wrong. Maybe your reason is that you must simply let them go to set yourself free. That was who you were then. You learned from it, but that is no longer who you are now.

Brené Brown, the bestselling author and shame researcher, teaches that anger is grief. You cannot forgive without grieving what you lost. It may mean coming to the realization that the person who you thought could never hurt you, did. Oprah said during a lecture that her forgiveness finally came when she decided to let go of the thought that the past could have happened any other way. And I love the way my friend and fellow coach, Tricia, puts it; she says she was finally able to come to forgiveness by seeing it this way: "Forgiveness was hard for me to get to with some of the situations in my life. Letting go was much easier, because then it felt like I was doing it for myself."

Before we continue to do any further work in this program, it is important that we clean the slate as we continue to move forward. We need to clear out what we don't want to make room for what we do want in our lives. You will not release everything all at once. It is a gradual process, but trust me, once you feel what freedom feels like, you will want to heal it and be free of it. For real, strong, resilient lovers, healing and releasing will become part of a regular practice to stay free, to keep your heart open, and remain resilient. As you continue to expand your awareness on this path, you will become even more resilient. Like a video game, you will keep leveling up. If the person you need to forgive hurt you over a long period of time, it may take time to feel healed. Be patient with yourself and allow yourself time. That is the most loving thing you can do for yourself.

How do you know when you are healed? When it no longer controls your life, and you no longer have a strong or debilitating reaction to it.

Remember, holding onto anger and resentment creates walls around our hearts that we think will protect us from hurting anymore; however, protecting our hearts also keep good things out like, love. If it's been a while since your break-up or since you've had a date, and you would love to have a beautiful, healthy, and loving relationship in the future, give yourself permission to heal, forgive, and open your heart for love to come in again. And remember, whoever hurt you doesn't deserve you staying devoted to them through your pain. Again, your best revenge is your own happiness and forgetting who they are, but remembering how it taught you to love and honor yourself more.

~ ~ ~

Relationships Are Assignments

To help us further understand why forgiveness is so important for our healing, personal growth and development, we must understand that life is a school and relationships are our assignments. However, in the school of life, you get the test first and the lesson later. This means every person and situation we encounter can teach us something about ourselves. Some people play small roles in our lives, while others have big roles. But sometimes there is no difference in the impression these people leave on us. Our teachers are also not only the ones we pick, but the ones the Universe brings to us to help teach us what we need to learn and understand. This means whatever you are experiencing right now is the lesson you need to propel you to the next level towards becoming your highest self.

These lessons can be on:

- Accepting yourself and others.
- Being compassionate to yourself and others.
- Not judging yourself or others.
- Being patient with yourself and others.
- Honoring yourself and others.
- Respecting yourself and others.
- Loving yourself and others.

- Forgiving yourself and others.
- Setting your boundaries and respecting others' boundaries.

Notice that all the lessons include "others." Healing is not just about you, healing also means how we treat others. During Marianne Williamson's farewell speech of her weekly lectures in New York City, just before she announced her presidential campaign in January 2019, she said, "If your healing only includes yourself and doesn't include others, you've only done half the work." Part of the reason we need healing *is* because of others. This practice is not only to help you heal but to help you to become aware of not passing your wounds onto others. Could you imagine what it would be like to live in a world where we all took responsibility of not passing our wounds and insecurities out on others? If we all contributed to the world's healing in this way?

The lesson of patience can show up in many ways with relationships. We may be impatient with a partner or become impatient waiting for a new partner. As the lessons show up in your life, if you continue to give it negative attention, rather than letting it go or trying to understand it through compassion, you will continue to create your own suffering. We have a lot more control over what we desire to feel than we realize.

When you try to run away from a lesson, such as not doing the inner work and healing your wounds, they will keep showing up in your life in different forms, situations, or people. The more we resist the lesson, the harder they will become because we get more frustrated. Once we understand the lesson, we discover the answer was within us all along. I have the power within myself to change my attitude and perception around this. When we see through the lens of love and understand the lesson, it can be a humbling experience or a huge epiphany. What you once thought was a curse can now feel like a blessing.

If you find yourself suffering, instead of asking, "Why me?" start asking yourself, "What can I learn from this?" Knowing that everything happens for us and not to us, we can begin to use these experiences as guides to help us grow. Most, if not all, lessons are teaching us how to love ourselves and others more.

Lessons can sometimes be quite painful. The Universe will literally bring us to our knees, because we are not listening. We actually bring it on ourselves, and it has to shake us to our core to show us what we refuse to acknowledge. I've always noticed that I experience the most growth from my most painful lessons. My lessons forced me to stop complaining and blaming and expecting others to do what I was not willing to do for myself, which was to honor myself. If I wanted something better for myself, I had to wise up and start taking responsibility and action. I discovered, when I finally woke up to that fact, it meant healing my wounds and loving and respecting myself. Heck, if you don't honor and respect yourself, no one is going to respect you either.

If you don't see yourself being treated with respect in a relationship, stop yelling, stop manipulating, stop trying to make them respect you. You have to learn to respect and be respectful of yourself. 1) When you respect yourself, you won't keep yourself in situations where you are not respected. 2) When you are respectful of yourself, you are respectful of others. Yelling at someone to be respectful to you, is not respect. You can't teach someone to be respectful of you if they keep showing you, they are unwilling to do it, and you certainly cannot teach someone to respect you by yelling at them. Put an end to your suffering, stop creating your own drama, and come to the realization that you have to honor and respect yourself by either removing yourself from situations that do not serve your highest good, and always be respectful to your partner when discussing issues. What you dish out is always reflected back to you. When you honor and respect yourself and others everything else will fall into place.

To prevent those type of relationships from happening again, I learned that I needed to heal myself first, so I didn't seek a partner to fill my voids or make my partner responsible for healing those wounds within me. Healing my wounds enables me to be a whole person with a partner who complements me, not completes me. I don't need to be with my partner; I want to be with my partner. There's a huge difference. Need is a total sell out of honoring yourself. Want is getting what you desire. Loving myself allows me to love my partner for who they are, not who I need them to be for me. What truer love is there than that? Healing my wounds and self-love enables me to get all the codependency, entanglements, and enmeshment fake-relationship BS out

of the way, so I can get to the real love I always wanted and deserved. That is what these relationship lessons are meant to teach you.

Painful lessons can crush those who refuse to understand or see there is a lesson behind it. They will continue to suffer. But, if they can learn from the lesson, they will become wiser, stronger, and more resilient. As I mentioned earlier, these lessons are not meant for us to be strong in the way our ego wants us to be strong, by building walls of protection around us. Its purpose is quite the opposite, which is to break down those walls of protection that ego builds up. Walls can also leave us retracting from life, distrustful of the world, and suffering alone.

Our toughest lessons are gifts in disguise from the Universe. Each lesson is meant not to defeat you, but to help you open your eyes. The Universe is trying to say, "When are you going to start loving yourself as much as I love you? When are you going to honor and respect yourself? When are you going to start seeing your worth? You deserve so much more than you are allowing." These lessons are to teach us that we are worthy of love; they teach us how to love ourselves; and they teach us how to love one another more. This is accomplished when we allow the healing wisdom of our higher self to come through.

~ ~ ~

We Are All Mirrors for Each Other

To understand how relationships are our assignments, it's helpful to look at our relationships as mirrors into how we feel about ourselves. What we feel about ourselves is reflected in our outer world, more specifically in all our relationships with coworkers, significant others, family, and friends. It is more apparent in our romantic relationships. The more we love and accept ourselves, the more we pick partners who truly love us. The less we love ourselves, the more we pick partners who do not love us or treat us well. The more we love ourselves, the more we are able to love and allow ourselves to be loved in return. How we feel about ourselves is a result of the depth and amount of our unhealed wounds.

Childhood Wounds that we avoid will continue to show up, even as we grow older. When we are unaware of our wounds, we look for partners to fill those empty voids inside of us to make us feel whole and worthy. I later learned this is what *A Course in Miracles* calls the "special relationship." When ego searches for someone to fill-up those voids and wounds within us to avoid suffering, but this person usually turns out to be your next lesson. We are subconsciously attracted to people whose wounds are as deep or deeper than our own. Thus, the person you thought was going to save you and fill all your voids with happiness, love, and self-worth, winds up being the person who makes you face all those unhealed wounds. That is what these painful, frustrating, dysfunctional relationships do—they mirror back our wounds; which gives us the ability (with self-awareness) to heal them. Healing doesn't always mean healing the relationship itself; many times, it means removing yourself from a painful and dysfunctional relationship, doing the inner work, knowing you are worthy of a healthy, loving relationship.

If you keep going back to someone who hurt you, your wound is telling you that you need this person to validate that you are worthy of love, rather than knowing you are already worthy of love. When you love and honor yourself, you won't tolerate bad behavior from anyone who is not being respectful of you and your love. As stated earlier, anytime we find ourselves fighting and trying to get someone to respect us, we are not respecting ourselves. Your worth is not something you fight for with someone else, it's something you already own.

Then there are those who want love so much, but they are so afraid to let love in. In this case, it's easier for them to have multiple, casual relationships, it gives them a false sense of empowerment and security rather than exposing their heart to one person who could hurt them. They won't put themselves in the position that could cause hurt. Or they date, people where they know they have the upper hand. The vast emptiness will remain, unless they address those wounds. If not, they will continue to self-protect by controlling and manipulating situations. They will get into relationships that make them feel in control. This could be because they have come from a tough, emotionally cold, or abusive childhood where they are survivors who will never be victimized again. Some were taught to be driven, that the world is a competition, and they must always come out on top. To these people, the world is made up of winners and losers.

Narcissists definitely fall into this category. Their behavior may superficially protect them, but it hurts so many others. Some people are so wounded, that their idea of love is distorted. Love is merely a commodity. The pain they inflict on others in an odd way makes them feel more loved. They have a hard time feeling empathetic towards you and the hurt they caused you. Somehow, you caused them to do it, or it's their painful childhood that caused it. This is why they don't feel remorse when they hurt people.

There is a wonderful quote by Stephen Chbosky, author of *Perks of Being a Wallflower*: "We accept the love we think we deserve." The more we understand and fill our wounds with love, self-validation and self-acceptance instead of looking for someone to fill them for us, the more healing we invite into our lives. The healthier and more whole you become, the less you will be attracted to or tolerate emotionally unhealthy people. The healthier and more whole you become, you will be more attracted to healthier partners, and they will be more attracted to you.

You and you alone are responsible for the people you allow into your life. You are also responsible for how much you accept and tolerate in a relationship. If you are in an unacceptable relationship, it's not your partner's fault. You are in charge of whether you remain in that relationship or choose to walk away. I've switched up the old adage, "Fool me once, shame on you. Fool me twice, shame on me," and changed it to, "Fool me once, shame on you. Fool me twice, still shame on you. I've learned my lesson, and I'm moving onto something better."

We Trigger People Too

One of my most life-changing revelations occurred when I became more aware of my own triggers, and at the same time, I began to see how I was triggering other people too. This can happen at any time with any person. We often don't know why we trigger people, but it will help us to understand that we do. It can cause a domino effect right down into the rabbit hole. The rabbit hole in *Alice in Wonderland* led her into another world. The rabbit hole of our ego is a chain of thoughts that cause our emotions to spiral downward.

My relationship with the guy I dated after my divorce triggered a lot of old wounds in me that I thought were healed. But with this practice, I was able to notice that I was triggering him too. We knew we triggered each other, but now with this new level of awareness, things were different. I began to realize that it wasn't that we simply weren't getting along. Triggering doesn't just mean we "upset" each other. Triggering means we are exposing each other's old stories and old wounds that are unhealed. We were still telling ourselves stories about not being good enough, feeling unlovable, and the fear of abandonment.

At first, I didn't realize I was hurting him. I only saw that he was hurting me. It wasn't only "not getting along" or "pissing each other off." Underneath, we were still two wounded kids. There is a beautiful, emotionally moving sculpture by Ukrainian artist Alexander Milov entitled, *Love*. It depicts two very large adult wire figures with their backs to each other and their heads down in misery, inside each adult is a child figure reaching out to the other for love. You may have seen it on social media, if not, it's worth looking it up. It is an amazing sculpture, representing the hurt child in all of us that simply wants to be loved.

I also began to observe that the moments when he would act cool and confident around me were actually when he was feeling the most insecure. And in typical guy fashion, he couldn't let me see that. So, in defense, he would act aloof towards me. Before I had this understanding, I would feel hurt, but now I can see through the mask right into the wound. Many of us have been there. We act calm, when in fact, we are dying inside, acting like nothing is happening. We fear appearing weak or vulnerable to the person we love, who could hurt us.

Being able to see his wounds made me feel like I had superhero-like powers. I didn't react with hurt or sulking behavior. Instead, it made me feel compassionate and empowered to say, "Hey, what's up? What's really going on here? When you do X,Y, and Z, it makes me feel_____." To my surprise, he responded differently than when I had my defenses up. He didn't feel he was being blamed or attacked, so he was more open to talk. Although we still had some heated discussions, the anger, deep hurt, and feelings of being misunderstood and unheard were gone. All of a sudden, he wanted to get on the

phone to talk things out instead of running away when I wanted to discuss something. Through these open discussions, I was able to find out there were so many more misunderstandings between us, because we were both quick to react and assume what the other was thinking, usually for the worst. That's how ego loves to work. Even though it didn't work out for many other reasons. We stopped fighting and started talking instead.

You Can't Change Anyone

It's extremely important for you to fully understand that if you want to have a successful relationship, you cannot change anyone, especially someone who doesn't want to change. You'll frustrate yourself trying. We also have no right to change anyone, just as they have no right to change us. Where do we get the idea that it's our right to change someone to suit us rather than accepting them and loving them for who they are? That's not love.

If you are in an emotionally abusive or toxic relationship with a partner who doesn't see a problem with their behavior, or who promises to change but doesn't, again, you and you alone are making the conscious decision to stay. The problem is not their unwillingness to change, it's your willingness to tolerate unacceptable behavior and stay in a negative environment. It's time to ask yourself why you are still in it? Why are you honoring someone who is not honoring you?

You think honoring yourself is saying, "I deserve more, so I'm going to demand him to change because I know I deserve better than this." You think you're in it to help him, but at the same time, you would be so out of there if you knew he didn't really love you? So, in effect, you're not really doing it for him but for what you can get out of it. You need him to change because you're afraid to move forward alone. However, with some people, their wounds are so deep there is no space for anyone else to be in their lives. Their relationship is with their addiction and with their wound.

So often, these relationships start off with intensity, passion, and fire, which is where you become attached. The person presents themselves as one way, to win you over. Once they have won you over, another side of them is revealed to you, and you wind up spending the rest of the relationship trying to change them back to who you thought they were at the beginning. The problem is, the foundation of the relationship was never real to begin with, but your two wounds were trying to fill each other's needs as quickly as possible to make the pain inside of you go away.

It has also been so ingrained in us to work on our relationships and not give up, especially in marriages. It is absolutely imperative that we work on our relationships through thick or thin, however, this does not apply if the relationship is toxic or abusive. All bets are off. It doesn't matter if you were married only two weeks. If there's emotional or physical abuse of any kind, there's nothing to work on, know your deal breakers and remove yourself from the situation. If you don't see any improvement, and you are cycling around; that may be the deal breaker. Know what works and doesn't work for you. Working on a relationship is deserved when mutual love and respect are present. If you're in an unhealthy, toxic environment, it doesn't matter how much you love them. It is not love or dedication to stay in it. It's abuse. You do not need to work on your relationship if your partner is toxically hurting you. You need to love and be dedicated to yourself first, and walk away.

If your relationship is not what you want and does not bring out the best in you, fight for yourself, your worth, and your vision. It's up to you to find someone who knows what love is and values love the same as you. But at the same time, in order to have that you have to learn to be attracted to what is good for you. Sometimes, there's a wound in you that makes you equate love with pain; it must be love if it hurts? Or it makes you believe that if love is too quickly won, and I'm not chasing it, it's too boring, and not interesting because you have been conditioned for drama. The more you love and heal yourself, the more these false, damaging beliefs that are getting in the way of what you want, will fade.

You Can't Save Anyone

Similar to the concept that you can't *change* anyone, you can't *save* anyone either. The most painful relationships usually happen because a wounded, empathetic heart meets someone who is even more deeply wounded, someone who may even describe themselves as "damaged"

and you want to save them from the pain. This person they want to save typically has had a heartbreaking childhood and experienced a lot of trauma growing up. Some people with painful childhoods are able to work through their pain towards finding healing and their life's purpose of helping others who suffer from the same trauma. However, so many still live their lives unconsciously in darkness, trying to run from their pain. You may want to help this person, because you love them so much, and you don't want them to hurt anymore. You want to save them from their mental and emotional anguish by bringing light and love into their lives. You believe love conquers all, and while this is true, they have already built a fortress around them to protect their fragile, broken heart.

This is a person who operates in survival mode due to their past experiences, and they have built up a lot of defenses. At times, they may seem loving and caring, but what you may not know is, they don't trust anyone enough to fully let them in. Your heart may go out to them when you hear that, still thinking that you could be the one to save them, because that's how much you love them. You don't mind, you are selfless after all. You can do this, but you will probably wind up breaking your own heart many times over. At some point, you have to ask yourself, "Am I loving this person at the risk of losing myself? Does this person care how much I love them? How much am I loving and honoring myself by staying in this? Does this person even love me back? Is this the relationship I want?"

You are allowed to be selfish and want love for yourself. You are allowed to be in a relationship of give and take. Healthy relationships are about give and take. Helping people does not mean martyrdom. Love does not mean martyrdom. The wakeup call is realizing this person is not capable of loving you in the way you want to be loved by them. It's okay to want love, we just have to become aware that we're doing it in a healthy manner. It's not selfish to want to be in a loving, respectful, and healthy relationship. You deserve it, but you have to be the one to get yourself there.

You most likely don't have the skills to help someone who may require the assistance of deep therapy. Even if you did have the ability, you have to ask yourself, "Do you want a partner or do you want a project?" As a coach, we are told during training, if we want to be successful (and keep our sanity), we have to know we can't save anyone. We are not saviors. That was really hard to hear at first, because it made me think, "Isn't that a little insensitive? What was the purpose of being a coach, if that wasn't what we are supposed to do? Was that just to let us off the hook, if we couldn't help someone?" When I started actually coaching people, it began to make more sense.

You can't shift the perception or raise consciousness in people who are not ready or also not willing to take responsibility for their lives. Some people say they are ready and still cannot see it. You can talk until you're blue in the face, and they will not get it, no matter how long you sit there or how many different ways you try to explain it. Some people aren't there yet. It's because it takes a certain level of self-awareness and an openness to understand. I know the first time I read, *Untethered Soul* by Michael Singer because I loved the title. I was on this spiritual healing path but I was not ready for that book because the entire book went over my head. Three years later, after finishing coaching school and doing a lot more inner work, I revisited the book, and it was a completely different experience. Everything made sense. This time, I thought it was an amazing beautiful book. This blew my mind.

Someone unhealed about something will most likely tell you that you don't understand. Most likely, they are stuck in the blame game, or they don't want to take responsibility for change, they want to be saved. People who want to be saved can't take responsibility because they don't know how to help themselves. They need you to do all the work for them, which involves you taking on a lot of responsibility for them to make sure they are happy and help them function in life. You are the life preserver they are holding onto. For them, that is the change they were hoping for in their lives, and it will be exhausting on their loved ones. Don't expect them to see things the way you do. They have a totally different mindset. They see life through a different filter. Their happiness and life are your responsibility. They may not act like it, but leave and their world fall's apart.

What they don't realize is that they've built a prison for themselves. Ego makes them think finding someone to take care of them sets them free, but being so dependent on someone creates a prison. If they are unhappy with their partner or wind up in a toxic relationship they

will be stuck in that relationship because they are dependent on that person for their survival. If both partners are dependent on each other, then they are in a co-dependent cycle. For the lucky ones, it's not until they hit rock bottom that they finally see the light. This is why recovery and healing groups say, "Don't deny anyone their rock bottom." They have to come to their own realization, not yours, which is why you cannot help anyone who is not ready to be helped.

We are all on different journeys. As someone who has stayed in relationships way too long before I found this practice, I always came to the point when I knew it was time to get out and save myself. I've always tried to learn what worked and what didn't work from my prior relationship so that I could make better decisions when choosing my next partner. As I've healed, I am now able to quickly identify a healthy or unhealthy match for me or a good or not so good match for me. In the relationship following my marriage, I saw things go from "best boyfriend ever" to recognizing seriously dysfunctional behavior. This was part of my lesson on this journey to see what I have learned. Behaving like he was the best boyfriend ever and moving the relationship extremely fast is a tell-tale sign of dysfunction. Rather than trying to stick around to make it work and help heal all his wounds for the next eight years, which is what I used to do, I loved and honored myself first. With that revelation, I got the hell out—fast.

Forgiveness and Boundaries

I can't write a lesson on forgiveness without mentioning something very important: Boundaries.

This one took a while for me to learn because I kept forgiving and allowing people in my life who really didn't deserve a place there. On the one hand, someone may have a hard time forgiving, while others forgive very easily, which society thinks it's not a good quality to have, but in personal and spiritual development world, it's what we want to achieve to let negativity go and to see things clearly. We all need to get into the habit of forgiving as much as possible, instead of holding onto resentment because it does lead to a happier, more peaceful life. However, one thing that sometimes gets left out in spiritual development is the need to set good healthy boundaries. When we forgive, there is also the tendency to let people who have hurt us back into our lives or not set proper boundaries with them.

There's a balance between recognizing our behavior too. When you are asking someone not to impede on your personal limits, then you have a right; however, if you're asking someone not to do something because it bothers you, like you don't like the way they do something, make sure you are not infringing on their rights. That's something you have to work out. Like the memes I keep seeing about, "Don't talk to me before I've had my coffee." Girl, that's your sh*t to work out, not their's. Keep yourself locked up in another room and meditate until you're ready to treat people without an attitude and with respect.

Forgiveness means letting go of what happened, putting it behind you and not harboring any resentment, so you can be free of it and move forward. It doesn't mean becoming a doormat or putting yourself in the same position to be hurt again with someone who does not respect you. Forgive, but learn to set your boundaries where necessary. Setting boundaries sometimes means loving some people from afar, especially those who continue to hurt you. Send them love and pray for their healing. Always honor yourself and your commitment to yourself first and foremost.

Our Thoughts Control Our Perception of the World

Have you ever gone to a scary movie and had those eerie jitters follow you home? Nothing has necessarily changed in your world, only your perceptions, because of the scary movie you saw. While our conscious mind knows it was just a movie, our subconscious mind cannot differentiate between reality and the fictional events from the movie. The subconscious believes what it saw was real, and it responds.

Our thoughts have the same effect on us. We play a scenario we create in our head, just like a movie, and we respond to it as if it were real. The truth is, like the movie, the majority of our thoughts are completely fiction. Our ego's thoughts are made up of a lot of false situations we merely assume. We assume we know what someone else is thinking and feeling, when in reality, we have no idea what

someone else is thinking and feeling, what it's like to be them, or how they came to make the choices they did. Ego loves to assume the worst. This makes ego feel smart, as if it is staying one step ahead and outsmarting the other guy. Again, this is ego trying to protect its fragile self from being hurt or disappointed, or anything that puts ego in the place of vulnerability. Ego wants to be superior, fully armored, and prepared. We predict outcomes and predict the worst. That is ego's fear filter. How many times have you let your thoughts escalate a situation? You become upset over beliefs you assumed, only to find out later it was a misunderstanding. Our thoughts can get us into real trouble, cause problems that aren't there, and make us so miserable over nothing. As Marianne Williamson says in *A Return to Love*, "Ego is suspicious at best. Vicious at worst."

Next time you are upset, pay attention to the quality of your thoughts and notice how they are influencing your emotions and mood. Then ask yourself, "How true is this thought?" These false thoughts can fill up our minds and seriously wreck our day, or even worse, drag us further into anxiety or depression clouding our entire vision of the world. Ego loves focusing on negativity, judging and blaming other people, while at the same time, ego's insecurity can make us feel like we're never good enough. This is why it is important that you are aware that these thoughts are not true; it's why you must know that *you* are not *your thoughts*, but the light within you trying to shine through. That is who you really are. Keeping ego at bay and staying connected to the light is a daily practice. Being mindful of the quality of your thoughts and what you are projecting out into the world and how it is affecting you will drastically improve your life and your relationships. If you find yourself in a negative downward spiral, try to reframe your thought to a loving one that serves you better.

Practicing mindfulness, meditation, and non-attachment help to quiet the mind's chatter and separate yourself from negative thoughts. The art of meditation and being present in the moment weaken the power that negative thoughts have over you. It's important to catch these thoughts in action before they take hold. Try to catch a negative thought as soon as you become aware of it. Witness it for what it is—a false story—and release and detach from it before it has a chance to take hold and produce a cyclone of thoughts that will drag you further down the rabbit hole.

Nipping these negative thoughts in the bud and catching it as soon as you have a self-defeating thought is much easier than undoing the damage these thoughts cause after you've been marinating your brain in it for a period of time.

Shining the Light on Darkness

We cannot heal our wounds, unless we are willing to face our darkness and shed light on it. That may sound scary to some of you, especially if you have been running away from your darkness for so long. But the more we are able face our fears, the less scary they become over time. However, it is important to take your time. If you have suffered serious trauma, you may want to do this with the help of a therapist who knows you are doing this healing work.

For others, the monsters are not as big as we imagined them to be, and sometimes like scared little children, we find our ghosts to be mere figments of our imagination. The revelation is similar to seeing a scary shadow created by an ordinary object on the wall. If you are scared to face your emotions, picture yourself as the reassuring adult or bring in an angel to protect you, if you believe in angels. See your adult self or your angel protecting your child self through the dark places you don't want to face alone during some of these exercises. Your adult self and angel will protect your inner child and send reassurance that you are safe.

Our Journeys

There is a beautiful meditation by Deepak Chopra from Oprah and Deepak's *Twenty-One-Day Meditation, Energy of Attraction*. On Day Seven: Your Deepest Desire, the mantra for this day is, "My deepest desire is to be complete." Being whole and complete is what we are working towards in this program. To heal and become whole and eventually meet the partner who complements you rather than needing someone to complete you.

I love this meditation because there is something in the music that moves me to my core. It makes me realize what a beautiful journey we are on. All of it—the good and the bad, the bittersweet. When we finally find the wisdom in our pain, then we realize, we wouldn't be who we are now without the lessons we have learned from it. How blind we were before this. How we thought this life was only about us. We come wanting things to improve our image with material things and people, to make us feel whole, but on this path, we learn that those are empty facades, masks, and fillers. We begin the healing work peeling off the layers, and what emerges reveals the light and beauty that existed within us all along. It is through the darkness that we find our light. And we discover that our purpose here on Earth is not for ourselves but to pass that torch and help others find their light.

~ ~ ~

Tools to Help You
Forgive and Release

(Use These Tools as Needed)

Non-Attachment, Reframing,
Surrender, Acceptance

You have been receiving many tools in this lesson, including journaling, setting intentions, and meditation. Tools are beneficial when we know how to use them. One of the most important things about using tools is knowing what tools work best for you, and what tools to use and when. As I mentioned in your Personal Growth Toolkit at the beginning of this book, it's important to learn how to balance tools. Tools like forgiveness need to be balanced with boundaries so you don't become a doormat. However, if we add too many boundaries, we become too fearful and protective. Adding too much non-attachment, we become void. Too attached, we lose control. The key is to always find your balance.

If you've achieved forgiveness, savor the freedom it brings. However, if you are having a difficult time or old stories and energies start popping up again, remember this is a practice. We're not looking for perfection. Perfection is part of the old story. Just pick-up where you left off, forgive yourself, and be mindful of how you could do it differently next time.

Non-attachment (detachment), surrender, and acceptance are wonderful tools to keep handy when you need to center and realign yourself with peace or love.

Affirmations and Intentions

These affirmations and intentions will give you an idea of the different type of affirmations and intentions you can add in your toolbox. The difference between affirmations and intentions are that affirmations affirm something you want to be or feel, and intentions for something you want to bring into your life or an action, but they can

be used interchangeably reciting them to yourself to get the desired results you want.

Feel free to adjust them to fit your situation. Affirmations and intentions only work if they resonate with you.

Non-Attachment Intention

Help to release the intensity of emotions

"I know my attachment to this is creating my suffering, so I release it."

Mindfulness Affirmations

"All that I need, I have right here and now."
"Being in the present brings me peace."
"I am not my thoughts."
"This too shall pass."

Surrender Intention

Help you to release you from what you are feeling.

"I surrender this to the highest good."

Reframing Intention

"I choose to see this differently."

Acceptance Affirmation

Acknowledge what you are feeling.

"I am enough."
"It's okay to feel what I feel."

Non-Attachment and Reframing

The practice of non-attachment is a wonderful tool to help you not get sucked down the rabbit hole. Non-attachment will help you stay present until that shift comes. Non-attachment and mindfulness are not about running away, but they help you distance yourself from your thought patterns and intense emotions. Part of non-attachment practice is knowing we place meaning on the people, places, and things in our lives. Remove the meaning, and you remove your attachment to it as well. Nothing has meaning until we give it meaning.

Buddhist philosophy believes all suffering is caused by attachment. The practice of non-attachment allows you to remain unattached to minimize suffering. We cause much of our own suffering when we become so attached to people, places, things, and to desired outcomes. We attach so much meaning to outcomes that when we don't get that particular job, or let's say an injury prevented you from doing something you love, and you become devastated. Some people never recover. They remain angry and bitter about what should have been. People who can release their attachment and even reframe it into something beneficial for them are the ones who thrive most in life.

The more you practice non-attachment to an outcome and reframing a situation to one that works for you, the easier it becomes to let things go and move on. It may not be easy when you are dealing with intense emotions, but it is still very effective with practice. As your mind drifts towards that person, a painful thought, or why things didn't work out the way you had hoped, bring yourself back to the present and energetically detach your emotions from that person or situation. When you become aware of energetically detaching your emotions from a person or a situation, you can literally feel the energy lifting and being released from you. Then reframe, and ask yourself, "How can I see this differently?" Be proud of yourself for the work that you are doing and how good it will be to finally be free of this and allow new and good things to come into your life.

Take a moment to try it now. Think about something you want to detach yourself from and say, "I choose to release myself from this situation," and feel your energy get lighter.

Repeat this throughout the day and notice the difference it has made.

Surrender

Surrender in a spiritual practice is different than what it means in modern society. Surrender doesn't mean "giving up." It's about releasing all that is not serving our highest good. We ask God or the Universe to "Please take this from me or help me to transform it. Help guide me through this." When you are on your knees in despair, surrender is probably one of the most helpful tools while you are already down there. It's also a useful tool if you are having a difficult time shifting or releasing thoughts and negative energy. Sometimes you may need a combination of surrendering, meditation, non-attachment, Yoga, and a walk in the park, to fully release.

As I mentioned earlier, I like to hit my yoga mat in child's pose and repeat this as often as necessary, until you finally shift and release it.

Acceptance

When you are having one of those moments where you feel absolutely horrible about yourself (we all have those days), the practice of Acceptance is a very effective tool. Just accepting what you are feeling, rather than resisting what you are feeling, is like releasing a pressure cooker valve. As humans, we have an automatic aversion to feeling bad, and this resistance makes us feel even worse. We have this false belief that we shouldn't feel bad, so we fight it, suck it up instead of accepting what we are feeling and listening to what our emotions are trying to tell us.

We place so much pressure on ourselves to fit in, to be successful, or to get things right, and we can beat ourselves up over it, constantly. This could be from an old childhood wound or having to do with the judgmental and competitive society we live in. Break away from this constricted thinking and know that you are enough. That is part of your practice, to remember that you are perfect, whole, and complete just as you are, and to remove any limiting beliefs that are holding you back from remembering this.

Society is uncomfortable with emotions; it makes us put on a mask and say, "I'm fine," when we're not, and pretend things are perfect when they're not. We're taught to keep up appearances, to fit in. We're controlled by what other people think. If we really want to be brave, radical, and authentic in this fearful society, then practice accepting yourself just as you are is the biggest middle finger. Acceptance is saying, "I am enough." "It's okay to feel what I am feeling." "It's okay not to be perfect!" "It's okay to be just as I am." What you are feeling is completely normal. Remembering that situational depression, anger, or resentment, are not places you want to stay for long periods of time, because you can become stuck.

Stop telling your friends you're okay when you are not. Ask or accept help when you need it. Talk to a therapist or a coach. Read a book on acceptance or do a meditation. Anything you can to stop and change the current tape that is running in your head telling you, you suck and you're not enough. Stop telling yourself you shouldn't be feeling what you are feeling and allow yourself to feel it. Close your eyes and take a moment to acknowledge what you are feeling and give yourself permission to feel. Place your hand on your heart and feel it. Really allow it to come up and breathe into the emotion. What is it trying to tell you what you need? Most of the time, it just needs love, attention, and to feel heard. Send love into that space and breathe into it. Tell it, "I hear you. I am here for you. I will not let you down." Allow it to flow through you, and out of you, to release it. Stop stuffing it down. The more you accept what we are feeling and give it the love and attention it wants from you, the less emotional and reactive you will be and the lighter you will feel.

Spiritual Bypassing

An enlightened practice is not what many people think, it's not about positivity. When you're not dealing with your shit, it's known as "spiritual bypassing." That's when someone doesn't want to do the inner work and only wants to shift into positivity. It's the person who stuffs crystals into her bra (I'm not against crystals, but there is a place for them in your practice) or burns sage to release negativity and thinks they're good to go. Then wonder why nothing is working?

Those things are lovely if you are using them with meditation, journaling, releasing, reframing, but they are not going to work effectively on their own. Yoga and meditation aren't even enough. You have to know what you are doing on your mat. You have to know what you are releasing and exploring in meditation. An authentic spiritual practice means having a deeper understanding of the practice, getting to the root and facing them head-on with love, compassion, and understanding to heal and release them. Avoidance is not releasing. It is in the healing that we feel lighter.

Sometimes going with the flow means not resisting darkness but nurturing it. Moving gracefully through the ebb and flow of life.

~ ~ ~

Forgiveness Healing Exercises

Forgiveness Affirmation: *"I forgive you. I release you."*

Forgiveness Music: "Long Time Sun," Snatam Kaur

Forgiveness Pocket Reminder: Your pocket reminder can be the words, "I forgive," or the affirmation, "I forgive you. I release you." Or, you can choose your own forgiveness affirmation, or anything to help bring you back to your forgiveness practice. Your pocket reminder is just a little token to remind you that you are honoring yourself and showing up for yourself every day.

Forgiveness Altar: Set up your altar with a candle, words, prayers, crystals, and affirmations that remind you of forgiveness.

Day 1: Forgiveness exercise: Write a letter to the person.

Affirmation: *"I am willing to forgive and release what is holding me back."*

For this exercise, you are going to write a letter to the person who hurt you to start the healing and releasing process. The purpose of this exercise is to release all the anger and hurt you have been carrying, maybe for a very long time.

Don't worry, you're not sending this letter. Energetically, they will receive your message, as we are all connected.

Free-write anything and everything you've been wanting to say. Write all the feelings you have connected to this person and situation to finally release them. You will probably feel many intense emotions come up during this exercise. Allow them to come up so you can finally let them go and be free of them. What's hidden cannot be healed. This exercise will also help you become aware of and release any hurt and anger you have been harboring, so you can be free of it and not carry it into your next relationship. It clears your heart and your energy to make way for real, healthy love.

Altar

Meditation ▪ Prayer ▪ Intentions

Light the candle on your altar or for meditation. You can also write out your intention and place it on your altar. Say a prayer, then sit in meditation (prayer is you talking to God and the Universe, and meditation is silencing the mind to receive guidance).

Sit for 5 to 20 minutes, creating awareness around what you wrote in your letter today, noticing if anything else comes up that you weren't aware of before. Become curious if you recognize any triggers. You may also use the free meditation I prepared for you on "Forgiveness," located on the Resilient Love website at:

karenOM.com/resilient-love-meditations
Password: resilientlover

Day 2: Forgiveness Exercise: Write a letter from the other person's perspective.

Affirmation: *"I am willing to see [name] as someone wounded, just as I am wounded."*

This exercise will help you understand the situation from the other person's point of view. Many times, when we are in a conflicting situation with someone, we become blinded with our point of view. This exercise will help strengthen your awareness and get you into the practice of seeing issues from all sides, until it becomes second nature to you. Analyzing a situation from the other person's perspective does not mean you agree with their behavior, if it was harmful to you. If your partner was emotionally or physically abusive towards you, because they had a tough childhood does not excuse the behavior. As an adult, your partner should be aware of their hurtful behavior and how to manage it so as not to repeat the cycle. Having awareness from both perspectives may help you to understand what happened between you.

Note: If there was abuse in your situation, this exercise on forgiveness is designed to help you gain awareness around the situation from the other person's point of view, only so it can be released, so you can let it go, clear it, and move forward from the harm it caused you. Be mindful that you not creating so much forgiveness that you put yourself in a harmful situation again with this person. It is important to forgive, but it is equally important to remember to set your boundaries and honor yourself as well. You may also choose to skip this exercise. Follow your heart. As you heal and love yourself more, you will no longer stay in situations where there is not mutual love and respect.

Forgiveness Journaling Exercise:

- Thinking from your higher self and using your intuition, what is it telling you about how the other person is thinking and feeling about this situation? Be honest about the situation, not what your ego wants to hear.
- Why did they do what they did?

- How much influence does their childhood wound have on their behavior?
- What fears may have been involved from their past?
- What other thoughts and insights are coming up for you about this situation?

Altar

Meditation ▪ Prayer ▪ Intentions

Light the candle on your altar or for meditation. Offer intentions for the highest good for all. Say a prayer, then sit in meditation from 5 to 20 minutes, creating awareness around what you wrote from their perspective today, noticing any shifts that may have occurred, and expanding your awareness around it. Become more curious about it. You can also use the free meditation I prepared for you on "Forgiveness" on my website.

Day 3: Exercise: Journal or Self-Observation on Your Thoughts

Affirmation: *"I am willing to see my part in this situation."*

Seeing Your Role

Sometimes, we get so blinded with being right, playing the victim and what someone else did to us, we don't see our role in how we participated in what happened? Being aware of the role we play, and our own toxicity, is one of the most enlightened things you can do to contribute to the health and well-being of your relationship. Great relationships don't just happen, they are created by two people who care about the state of their relationship and the treatment and well-being of their partner. Being honest with yourself is the first step. Did you contribute to the deterioration of your relationship? In what ways do you recognize this? Women can be emotionally and physically abusive, too. How can this recognition help you create better relationships in the future?

Relationship toxicity check list:

- Do you have a bad temper?
- Do you shout and yell?
- Do you name-call?
- Do you give your partner "the silent treatment"?
- Are you vengeful?
- Do you punish to teach your partner a lesson, or do you manipulate to get your way?
- Are you passive aggressive?
- Do you do malicious things to hurt your partner without owning up to it?
- Do you expect your partner to "just know things" without any form of communication or clarification?
- Do you treat your partner as if they were an idiot?
- Have you tried to change them into who you wanted them to be?
- Do you make them responsible for saving you or making you happy?

Maybe your part was picking the wrong partner or staying in the relationship too long, but the more you recognize your role in a relationship, the healthier and happier not only will you be, but your future relationships will be as well.

Today, you are going to write about the ways in which *you* were accountable.

Forgiveness questions:

The way we heal is by witnessing how our wounds and triggers are showing up in relationships, then acknowledge them so we can shed light on them to release and heal them.

- What role did you play in what happened?
- What old wounds from the past may have come up and triggered you?
- Do you notice any patterns you are repeating in your relationships? Do you keep choosing the same type of unavailable or abusive partner?
- How will witnessing the role you played help you create better relationships in the future?

Altar

Meditation ▪ Prayer ▪ Intentions

Light the candle on your forgiveness altar and sit in meditation, expanding your awareness on the role you played and what changes you want to bring in now to create better relationships in the future. Set your intention, offering this situation to the highest good. You may also write your intention and set it on your altar or pray: "God, please help me to see the role I played in this relationship and past relationships. Please help me see my own harmful patterns that are not serving me, my partners, or my relationships well. Please help bring them to light so that they may be healed, and I may create better, healthier, more loving relationships for myself in the future."

Day 4: Forgiveness Exercise: Journal or observe your thoughts on forgiving the person.

Affirmation: *"I am willing to accept [name] as someone on his/her own journey."*

Today, you are going to finally journal about forgiving this person. We needed to go through the process of releasing your hurt and anger, trying to see things from the other person's perspective, and your role in it, so you could have a better understanding on why you are forgiving them, even if the forgiveness is for *you*. You may want to include how this forgiveness is for you in your writing today. If you are still having trouble forgiving, it's okay. Accept where you are. Take baby steps. Continue releasing and surrendering this situation to the Universe, asking your higher self or the Universe to help you release it and shed new light on it. It may require you to look deeper into how ego might be showing up and standing in your way. Remember, ego likes to keep you in victim mode. Your higher self is wise and sees all. This is what we are trying to connect with, so true healing can occur.

Forgiveness questions:

- Through your writing exercises, what are you able to forgive now that you weren't able to forgive before?
- What were both of your roles in this?
- How were you both triggered?
- What do you think this relationship came into your life to show you?
- In what ways did the relationship help you evolve?
- What do you know now about yourself that you didn't know then?
- How will this help you in the future and in future relationships?

Altar

Meditation ▪ Prayer ▪ Intentions

Light the candle on your forgiveness altar and say in prayer, "God, please help me heal from this relationship and forgive, so I may release it. Please help me understand its purpose, so I may be healed, be free, and move forward."

You can also use the meditation I created for you on my website at:

karenOM.com/resilient-love-meditations
Password: resilientlover.

Set your intention and offer this situation up for the highest good for all.

Day 5: Forgiveness Exercise: Journal or observe your thoughts on giving thanks to your teachers

Affirmation: *"Thank you, [name], for being my teacher."*

You may feel great after the exercises you completed on days 1 to 4. It may feel like a huge emotional weight was lifted off you if you were able to release a lot of old feelings and put a fresh perspective on your situation. But if you are still feeling some residual negative energy after these exercises, that is completely normal too. Painful experiences can take time to shift and release. If your perception still has not shifted, continue setting your intention on your willingness to see it differently, and keep trusting a new perspective will come to you.

Be open to receiving. Many times, we are so caught up in ourselves we set an intention or say a prayer, but then don't see the signs that are in front of us. Trust and stay open. Today, you are going to write about, giving thanks. Yes, you are giving thanks to this person for coming into your life and teaching you what you needed to heal from the past for greater personal growth.

(If you've had a particularly difficult or abusive relationship, you may skip this exercise. You never have to thank someone who was abusive towards you, but you can thank yourself for what you learned from it and how it taught you to never to be in an another abusive relationship again and break the cycle of toxicity and dysfunction).

Forgiveness questions:

- In what ways can you be thankful for this person coming into your life? What good things did they teach you, if any?
- What did this relationship or this person show you about yourself that you would not have known had they not come into your life?
- In what ways can you be thankful for the lessons this relationship taught you?
- How did it make you a better person or teach you how to be a better partner or choose better partners?

Altar

Meditation ▪ Prayer ▪ Intentions

Light the candle on your altar and sit in meditation or prayer. "Thank" this person for coming into your life and honoring their Universal assignment with you. If you can't "thank" this person, try being thankful for the lesson you received from them that will help you move forward. If you like, write an intention and set it on your altar. When you forgive someone, you energetically release the tension and create more peace in your life and on earth.

Day 6: Forgiveness Exercise: Journal or observe your thoughts on how becoming aware of mindfulness tools has helped you in your healing.

What shifts do you feel?

- Which tools were most effective for me and why?
- How did I use Non-Attachment, Reframing, Surrender, and Acceptance?
- How can I see mindfulness as being a useful tool in my practice?
- What steps can I take to keep up with this practice?

Altar

Meditation ▪ Prayer ▪ Intentions

Light the candle and sit in meditation or prayer and choose to focus on non-attachment, surrender, or acceptance. Set your intentions on what you want to bring more of in your life: non-attachment, surrender, or acceptance.

If you would like to learn more about mindfulness, there are so many wonderful books to choose from. Two of my favorites are, *Untethered Soul*, by Michael A. Singer, and *Radical Acceptance*, by Tara Brach. I highly recommend any audiobook by Tara Brach. Listening to them is like listening to a peaceful, serene meditation.

Day 7 Forgiveness exercise: Journal or observe your thoughts on forgiveness questions.

Affirmation: *"My lessons are gifts in disguise."*

Throughout the day, think about the progress you made this week and reflect on it. What are your new stories?

Forgiveness questions:

- How has or can forgiveness help me heal?
- How has or can forgiveness set me free?
- How do my new stories empower me vs. my old stories?
- What are my new beliefs?
- What are some steps that I can take to keep myself aligned with my new beliefs?

Altar

Meditation ▪ Prayer ▪ Intentions

Light the candle and sit in meditation or prayer on your new story. Set an intention on your new beliefs and your commitment to them and to yourself.

~ ~ ~

You've made it to the end of this week's assignment. I know this isn't an easy process, but I promise it will be so worth it. I bet you are already seeing some huge shifts and amazing benefits and there will be more. Be proud of how much you are showing up for yourself! That alone is proof of your self-love, knowing you deserve and want something more for yourself.

Focus on celebrating yourself before you move on to the next lesson. You're going to also start getting into the habit of celebrating yourself and your achievements. We often forget to celebrate ourselves for our accomplishments. Celebrate yourself in any way your soul feels called to do.

Go buy yourself a new essential oil or crystal because you did the work. Treat yourself to an acai bowl, go to yoga and set your intention on being proud of you and celebrating you! The purpose is to be mindful of celebrating you and all of the work that you did!

Use this time to reflect on your new stories, your healing, and your growth. You can also start developing your own practice.

Self-Forgiveness/ Self-Compassion

*Today I will choose not to judge myself,
but be kind to myself*

Forgiving Ourselves

Sometimes, it's easier for us to forgive others than it is to forgive ourselves. We can be our own worst enemies. In most cases, we wouldn't talk to our best friends the way we talk to ourselves. Your inner voice could be the result of your environment growing up. If you grew up around perfectionists or critical people, you may have unconsciously picked up their habits, which became a part of your own inner voice and critic. As in the lesson on Childhood Wounds, this is not to place blame on your parents or caregivers, or anyone else for that matter. It is only to bring awareness around how we came to believe what we believe so we can reframe it to something that works better for us. As you know now, blaming doesn't serve us well, anyway. It only puts the power in their hands and makes us more resentful and angrier. Remember, they too were handed down these beliefs and behaviors by their parents and caregivers. We're ending the cycle to create a happier and more peaceful life for ourselves.

Maybe you feel like you really screwed up with a friend or a boyfriend. Maybe you think that if you acted or behaved differently, then things would have been different? Maybe you're mad at yourself, thinking, "If only I were confident enough, pretty enough, not needy, or thin enough, we'd still be together." If you think you had to be prettier or

thinner to keep someone, they didn't deserve you. Sure, we all need to do the inner work, but if you did your best, trust me, there's nothing different you could have done. It was meant to be. It's good that they're gone so now you can bring in someone who does see your worth.

Whatever you are having a difficult time forgiving yourself for, remember: *You are enough.* Thinking you're not enough is what keeps us stuck, and it also keeps us from feeling good about ourselves. When you don't feel good about yourself, you don't have the energy or desire to move forward. Feeling inadequate comes from the way we were conditioned, but it is not the truth of your real value. The cosmetics and the beauty magazine industry make billions of dollars based on our feelings of inadequacy. They convince us that their products will "improve" us, because we're not good enough as we are, and every year, they present another new trend that we "must" buy or do in order to keep up and fit in. We pride ourselves on our uniqueness and individuality while doing everything to fit in. Unfortunately, we fall for it. But we will get more into that in our lesson on self-love. Right now, keep remembering that you are perfect just as you are, and you are enough. Don't let anyone else tell you otherwise.

However, maybe you're the one who hurt your former partner, and your partner couldn't find a way to forgive you, and you're beating yourself up and continuously punishing yourself over it. If you tried apologizing but were not forgiven for something that was an honest mistake, it's more about their wounds than it is about you. They may have experienced a lot of pain and mistrust in the past. They may have trouble forgiving because they are protecting themselves from ever being hurt again. Don't beat yourself over it, but rather pray that you both receive what you needed from the lesson and move on. Know and trust who is meant to be in your life will be in your life, and who is meant to go, will go. If it was a repeated mistake or one where you breached their trust, then it's time to be honest with yourself, that was your lesson to learn and they are now setting their boundaries. Trust is like glass; once it's shattered, it's very hard to repair it back to its original state. It's natural to feel bad but learning from it, and changed behavior is much better than wallowing in self-pity and guilt.

Finding purpose in your mistake, and having it make you a better person, serves you and your future partner(s) much better than carrying that resentment and guilt into your next relationship and unintentionally hurting the next person. Your new relationship deserves your attention without open wounds from the past. The purpose of your former relationship was for you both to learn lessons, no matter what they may be, the lesson comes from you and who you were at that time and with that person. Say a prayer and thank them for coming into your life to teach you this lesson. Tell them you are sorry they were hurt in the process, pray for their healing and growth, as well as your own, and send them love.

Now, give yourself permission to move on from it. Sometimes that's all we need, is to give ourselves permission, knowing it was part of our Universal lesson for growth. Awareness is the path to freedom and happiness. We all mess up from time to time, but it's how we decide to show up differently in the future that makes all the difference. Every new day is another chance for change. When we change ourselves, we can change our lives.

~ ~ ~

What We Believe Becomes Our Reality

What we think about ourselves and what we say to ourselves is who we *become,* and we project that image out onto the world and into our relationships. We see the world based on the filters we project. These filters form our experiences, so if we had an experience that left us feeling unlovable or inadequate, we will believe we are unlovable or inadequate. We will also believe that the world or our partners see us this way as well, and we will subconsciously look for evidence to support that belief, even if it is far from the truth. Our fear-based egos are so slick and think it's so clever. We see what we want to see, and we will make it true. That is one way the world is an illusion we create through our perception.

Take a look at the beliefs some men and women have. Some women think, "All men are jerks," while some men think, "All women think men are jerks." Someone who holds onto one of these as a strong belief may have had several experiences that confirmed it to be true.

Understandably, they will start believing this is how all men or women must be since this has been their experience. It is through this belief that a filter of perception is created, and they may start seeing evidence to support that belief because that is where their focus is on now. Our egos love to be right. Someone with these beliefs may unknowingly self-sabotage or presumably treat men as jerks, or be defensive of women because the egoic fear-based mind sees what it wants to see as right but also wants to protect them from any future hurtful experiences. Thus, creating the reality that shows them that men are jerks or all women think men are jerks.

Men and women who do not share this belief will sense this energy coming from them, and in turn, will respond in defense. Both parties may be completely unaware this is going on, but it becomes a cycle of cause and effect. This also creates a "self-fulfilling prophecy." You fear something so much, you actually make it happen. This is how we create our own reality and how we experience the world differently than others. So if you want to create something, make sure to make it something good that works for you, and not against you.

Energy Grows Where Your Focus Goes

This is true of any belief we have, positive or negative. We all do it. Negative beliefs, which are known as "limiting beliefs," could have originated from our parents and care takers. Maybe they communicated a belief that money was difficult to earn and keep. A negative belief could have also come from a bad experience, which resulted in the incorrect assumption that because something happened once or several times, it will happen again. Let's say you are a woman who doesn't like approaching guys first, because so far, every time you have in the past, you got rejected. Guys experience this throughout their dating lives, but they keep trying until they meet someone who is interested in them as well.

The guys who are most successful at dating are the ones who don't adhere to that rule. They don't let rejection, or a negative situation stop them. They keep trying. They become *Rejection Proof*, which is a really fun read by, Jia Jiang, by the way. Negative beliefs about your self-worth may give you a false sense that good things will never happen to you, because you're just not "lucky." It's the, "I can't do it" or "I don't deserve it" thinking. The more you focus on a negative belief, the more it becomes your truth, but that does not mean it is *the* truth. Make sense? Stop for a moment and let that sink in. Limiting beliefs can really hold us back from living our full potential and achieving the life we deserve.

On the other hand, forward action beliefs or positive beliefs have the opposite effect. They give us the motivation to move forward. If you want to create positive change in your life, it's important to understand what your limiting beliefs are, no matter where they came from, and recognize how they are holding you back. You have to witness your ego in action and get out of your own way.

Acknowledging, creating an awareness, and changing your perception around your limiting beliefs will help you tremendously in overcoming them. Try reframing your beliefs to ones that work for you rather than against you. The purpose of reframing a negative belief isn't only about making you feel better; it is also about shifting your perception of a situation so you can move forward from it. When we are in a positive state of mind, we allow ourselves to become open to receiving. We are able to connect to our inspiration for guidance, and we align ourselves with abundance, opportunities, and possibilities. We are connected to truth. Remember, all of us are always doing our best from our current level of awareness. Everything comes to us at the perfect time we need it.

There's No Such Thing as Failure

No one is born a success. J.K. Rowling, who went from welfare to billionaire, is a prime example. She was rejected by twelve publishers before she found one that agreed to publish her first Harry Potter book. Oprah, the highest-paid woman on TV, was told by her boss that she was not right for television. The Beatles were rejected by Decca Records, because they didn't like their sound and said they had no future in show business. What if these people had stopped at the point of rejection and refused to move past other people's opinions?

That is the difference between successful and people who don't succeed. Successful people are so passionate about what they are doing, they believe so much in what they are doing, they move beyond the disapproval of others. Even if one door closes, they will keep trying until they find that one open door. If you want to succeed in your life and in your relationships, you must do the same. Always look for solutions rather than focusing on obstacles.

The only difference between you and someone you believe has it all, is *their beliefs*. Successful people form their beliefs around what they want to achieve, and in most cases, they have failed many times before they succeeded. But the key to their success was their willingness to keep going. We only see the results but have very little understanding about what they had to go through to get there. Go check out earlier videos of successful people and see how much they have improved over time. We can learn so many great lessons from our so-called failures. It's just another opportunity for growth.

This week, you are going to forgive all your limiting beliefs, because seriously, by your very nature, you are human. You have them. And you are going to start re-training your mind towards a growth mindset. The goal is to work your way through your limiting beliefs and bypass any perceived obstacles you have around your healing and around your relationships that are keeping you stuck. Forgiving yourself for having these limiting beliefs, and choosing a belief that works for you and moves you forward (even if it means you need to rest to keep going), are important parts of this practice.

How does this all fit in a lesson on self-forgiveness, compassion, and relationships? We can be so hard on ourselves. When we don't feel good and are unforgiving about ourselves, we unknowingly take it out on our partners, and in some cases, blame them for it. When we don't feel good about ourselves, we have a hard time loving others and allowing them to love us. The bottom line is that in order to have a healthy relationship with others, we must have a healthy relationship with ourselves first. Your relationship with yourself is by far your most important relationship. It sets the foundation for your emotional and mental well-being. Does this mean we need to be perfect? Absolutely not. Perfectionism is actually the root of many problems and also a limiting belief that does a lot more harm than good.

There's no Such Thing as Perfection

Of course, perfectionism exists, but *perfection* itself is an unattainable illusion created by man. To be "perfect" means to be completely free of faults or defects. Not one of us here on earth is perfect, but at the same time we are all perfect as we are. We can say God is the only being who is perfect, yet there will be someone who will say, "How can there be a God when the world is so imperfect?" That's not to say God is not perfect, but to illustrate how perfection, like beauty, is in the eye of the beholder. In a spiritual practice, God is perfect and so are we, it is we who do not see ourselves as perfect. The definition of perfection is different for everyone. Someone may say the perfect place to live is in the city, while someone else will say it's in the country. The perfect vacation is on a tropical island; the perfect vacation is exploring foreign cities. There is nothing in this world that is everything to everyone. We can say tacos are the best food ever, yet there will be someone who says they hate tacos. (I know. Crazy, right?)

Brené Brown, the author of *Gifts of Imperfection*, explains that perfectionism is a mechanism we use to try to prevent others from judging us. However, by striving for perfection, we have unconsciously built a life around those wounds of criticism, rather than preventing other people's judgments, perceptions or approval to have control over us, the perfectionist does it to themselves. This is ego at work again. The inner talk of a perfectionist is self-criticism. We hear all the time that we are our own worst enemy. We don't realize how much harm we do to ourselves by entertaining our crazy inner talk that constantly judges and compares us to other people. When you are so fixated on how everything looks to others, pleasing everyone else and meeting their approval, you leave little to no room to be yourself. Most perfectionists are exhausted—exhausted from competing with themselves and others, exhausted from the hours they put in, and exhausted from the stress of avoiding what they are feeling. Our awareness of how perfectionism affects our lives allows us to free ourselves from the effects of perfectionism.

You'll notice when perfection is impacting your life when you are focused on the exteriors of how things look, how things sound, how they are presented. How they reflect on you. You are looking for

perfection, instead of substance of what really matters in life. This is ego still getting in the way, focusing on what isn't important. You see it all the time—maybe someone posts a great inspirational quote on social media, but it has a typo in it. A hundred people will get the meaning of the quote, but there are always a few stragglers who can't see past the typo and into the beauty because they are fixated on pointing out the flaw to everyone.

On YouTube, there will be an amazing meditation with hundreds of people leaving delightful comments, but then there is the one person who says, "The sound quality wasn't that great." Ego prides itself on noticing these imperfections. It makes the ego feel superior. However, the people on this path who have done the work don't even see trivial things anymore; they are focused on the love, the meaning, and on what really matters. They focus on what is *good*. They don't let unimportant things get in the way anymore.

Competition

What if I let you in on another little secret? There is no such thing as competition either. Say what?

Competition, like perfection, is also an illusion created by our ancestors out of survival and fear. It doesn't mean it doesn't exist—it does, because we make it so. The Universe has created a perfect environment for us. There is enough to go around. What stops it from going around is ego, competition, and greed and our illusions of it.

An example of how competition is a limiting belief, my friend Ruth, started raising honeybees in her backyard in Douglaston, NY to help support the declining bee population worldwide. A few months later, the head of the company she worked for retired and closed the business leaving Ruth without a job. Having four kids to raise and two heading off to college, Ruth quickly shifted gears and started putting her honey into lip balms and selling the honey in small, personalized bear-shaped bottles. Today, she has a thriving retail business both online and in stores. One day Ruth and I were having lunch in Brooklyn; I told her I was contemplating leaving the corporate world to become a solopreneur as a coach, but friends keep forewarning me not to do it, saying it's too risky. She said, "Karen, if I had listened to everyone who told me I shouldn't sell lip balms or honey because there were so many companies doing it already, I wouldn't be here." Her business has continued to grow over the years and even expanded into honey-infused skin care products. People will say the market is saturated, but the moment something new comes out, we're excited to try it.

This is an excellent example that there is enough business to go around. If you are willing to take a chance and develop a good product. One of the key things to Ruth's success in business she said, "You know that voice in your head that tells you stop and not do something?" She said, "I don't have that voice. I keep going then figure it out how to make it work later on." And she does always find a way to make things work. Stop listening to the naysayers who say it can't be done. They are only speaking of their limitations. Don't look at what other people are doing if it's psyching you out. Find a way for it to be done.

I love this quote from Brené Brown's audiobook lecture, *Power of Vulnerability*: "Comparison is the thief of joy," Theodore Roosevelt. It took me nearly 40 years to learn about this powerful quote. It took me nearly 40 years to learn about all these life changing tools I am sharing with you in this book.

These are the type of lessons we should learn in school. I have never in my life used algebra outside of school. But how many of us willingly give up our joy for comparison every day. Seriously, how miserable do we make ourselves? And that habit has got to stop, right now if you want to be happy. We give up our joy, our passion, our self-worth, and our value, every time we compare ourselves to someone who we think is doing better than us. In turn, we try to make ourselves feel better by judging and criticizing other people who we think are not doing as well as us, "At least I'm not that girl. I must not be so bad." Or if ego does think they are doing better than you, then it gets super catty. It looks for anything to take her down so we don't feel bad about ourselves, "Who does she think she is?" "Omg, did you look at that dress?" I think we all know what it's like to be unfairly or ridiculously judged and it sucks.

Ego will make enemies of people who are not our enemies. We have to stop allowing ego to drag people down to lift ourselves up. Ego is in jealous mode when you hear such statements as, "Oh, they may look like the perfect couple on IG, but you have no idea what's going

on behind closed doors." You know what? No relationship is perfect, but maybe they are pretty freaking happy behind closed doors too. Their unhappiness shouldn't make you feel better about your life. Instead, try looking at their love and happiness to give you hope that real love and happiness do exist, and it will happen for you. Look at them as what's possible for your relationship goals like a living vision board, and if you can't, then look at them as people who are on their journeys, just as you are on your own.

The competition/comparison ego mindset puts us in a lower vibration of thinking, making us act in small ways. It pits us against one another, one-upping each other and always trying to catch other people's imperfections and worse, calling them out on it. It's a bad habit that makes us look bad and others feel horrible. A growth mindset doesn't see others as competition but sees opportunities and ways to collaborate. It seeks to support others as a community where there are no winners or losers, everyone wins.

Other ways comparison considerably robs us of our joy is when we compare things and places to the best. We pride ourselves on having such discriminating taste. We love being unimpressed! We wear it with pride. When, in reality, all that's doing is killing more of our joy. When you are constantly comparing things to the all-time best, you lose everything you can enjoy in the moment. No wonder we're unhappy. We're always looking for that next big fix. When we are always comparing things to the best, it's probably not going to meet your approval majority of the time. Sure, there will always be places that don't vibe with you here and there, but they will be fewer and farther in between. It's when most places or events aren't vibing with you that you are having trouble being satisfied with anything. That's when you know you are experiencing a problem. When you are always comparing and looking for what's wrong, you are always going to find it. Rather than looking for what you can enjoy and appreciate in the moment.

I love the story Tara Brach shares in her book, *Radical Acceptance*, of when the Dalai Lama was asked by a reporter, "What would you say was the best moment of your life?" and he responded, "This moment, right now."

The majority of people are not even aware of the judgmental movie silently running the show in the background of their mind. They also aren't aware of the long-term effects of self- criticism. They've been feeling miserable for so long; they don't know or remember what it was like to feel good anymore.

What if you could pursue everything you want in life without all the life-sucking stress of self-criticism? Self-criticism can happen a lot when we are healing from a relationship or in-between relationships. We place a lot of judgment on ourselves, on others, and in the process. Instead, exchange criticism for passion and pursue your joy, not focusing on other people's perceptions or approval or even your own approval. To get there, you have to be willing to continually release the mental grip that egoic fear tries to get a hold on you. Continue focusing on how something can inspire you and on all of the opportunities around you. Tell yourself, life is good and it will be good.

Let go of the perfectionism, the self-criticism, the self-judgment. Let go of comparing yourself to other people. Let it all go and forgive yourself for what happened in the past and for not knowing what you did not know sooner. Every day is a new day to learn from and start again. Then, if someone does criticize or judge you, you'll remember what it was like when you were judgmental and critical. Have empathy. Wish them healing and love, and move on. The more you become aware, the less you take things personally. You know now that feeding into competition shows where the other person still needs healing. So, if you absolutely must be perfect at something, strive for being "perfectly imperfect" and loving yourself as you are.

Ending this vicious cycle of comparison and competition is another step in freeing ourselves from the madness, and helping the world heal and evolve.

~ ~ ~

Perception Exercise—Part 1

This is a quick exercise in perception. Take a look around, wherever you are, for everything that is red. Take a good look and memorize the items. When you are finished, view the results of this exercise in the box below.

Perception Exercise Results—Part 2

Now think back at everything you saw that was blue around you. Can you remember any blue items without looking for them?

This is how our perception works. What we see is where we place our focus. We don't see what we don't put into focus. Because you were focusing on red items, you didn't even notice the blue items around you. What you focus on, you'll see more of in your life. If you want to see and feel more love in your life, you have to focus on *seeing* and *being* more love. If you want to continue this exercise further, do this throughout your day with blue cars or blue shoes or any blue item. You won't believe how many blue things you see now that it's in your awareness.

~ ~ ~

Self-Compassion

Self-Compassion Leads to Resiliency and Better Self-Esteem

There is a huge misconception that confidence is the same as high self-esteem. The two are not the same. There are a lot of confident people who silently suffer from low self-esteem and depression. They have a tough exterior, but inside, they don't feel good about themselves. Most don't even like or love themselves. Kristen Neff, author of the book, *Self-Compassion*, talks about the popular theory in the early 1990s of raising children to be confident. Parents told their children they were "great," and they were the "best," with the belief this would give their children strong confidence to help them succeed in life. Teachers gave gold stars to everyone, so no one failed. While these strategies were well-intentioned, they didn't have the desired effects. These children did develop high self-confidence, but many also developed narcissism. As the children grew, it was discovered they lacked the coping skills and self-esteem to handle failure. All their self-esteem and self-worth were directly tied to their success. They never learned how to handle failure. When they did fail on college exams, sports, or anything else, they got angry and had a difficult time recovering from failure. Instead, they became depressed and expressed little interest in trying again. They could not bounce back. High self-confidence and positive re-enforcement did not make them resilient.

The children were raised to believe they were winners; thus, failure was not supposed to happen to them. The results were not at all what child experts and parents had anticipated. It was devastating. Through Neff's research on self-compassion, she however discovered that children who practiced self-compassion also developed healthy self-esteem, and confidence came more naturally to them. When they failed, they were able to bounce back and try better next time. Self-compassion also teaches us to be more compassionate towards others. When we are compassionate and understanding of ourselves, we are able to be more compassionate and understanding of others.

Negative Inner Talk Affects Your Well-Being

Are you ever in a crappy mood but don't know why? Check your ego's inner self-talk. There's a good chance it's the main culprit dragging you down. As you now know, our thoughts can change our perception on the world like a filter. Our thoughts also affect how we are feeling. If we are feeling negatively about ourselves, of course it's going to drag us down. And when we feel negatively about ourselves, we'll also believe others feel the same way about us.

Brené Brown talks about knowing the difference between shame self-talk and healthy self-talk. Healthy self-talk says, "*I messed up*," versus shame self-talk, which says, "*I am* messed up."

Healthy self-talk focuses on the action. Shame self-talk focuses on the person. Whatever we place after "I am" is what we think and believe we are. Shame self-talk significantly lowers self-esteem since our subconscious is always listening and believes everything we think. Which is why if you're going to believe what you think, think good things. The best way to combat negative inner talk is with compassionate self-talk, as shown in the following exercise:

Self-Talk Exercise—Part I: Negative

Close your eyes and say the following statement, "What was I thinking? I'm such a complete idiot. Everyone probably thinks I'm an idiot too. How could I have done such a stupid thing? I'm such a screw up!"

Notice what emotions come up for you? How you are feeling?
The feelings you have now are the effects of negative self-talk.

Self-Talk Exercise—Part II: Compassionate

Now, this is the same scenario, but this time, you're going to use compassionate self-talk. Close your eyes again. Say to yourself,

"You know what? Yeah, I did screw it up. Everyone makes mistakes. I tried. Successful people try and fail all the time. Hey, at least I tried and I can learn from this. I'm definitely not going to make that mistake again. I'll do better next time. There's always another way."

Notice the difference between how you feel with negative self-talk and compassionate self-talk.

Both are the same situation, but you likely notice the difference between the types of self-talk and how your mood shifts when you are beating yourself up vs. being compassionate to yourself. Notice how negative self-talk can not only harm your self-esteem and make you a victim, but change the course of your life. Negative self-talk makes you reluctant to move forward, whereas compassionate self-talk recharges you and helps you to move forward towards what you do want to achieve in life. Negative self-talk makes you feel heavy and lethargic; compassionate self-talk makes you feel lighter and freer. The person with negative self-talk may be stewing at home, sleeping and binge drinking. It may feel goofy at first (your ego getting in the way), but the person with compassionate self-talk has moved on and is already working on something new.

Always pay attention to the quality of your thoughts and be sure to address negative self-talk with loving kindness and compassion. For further information on being more compassionate to yourself, read *Self-Compassion* by Kristen Neff.

~ ~ ~

Everything Happens as it Should

Have you ever had something happen, then weeks, months, or years later, you understand why everything happened the way it did? You realize that the situation brought you to your current point in life. I always felt this way. I've always noticed that a certain job led me to the next job or how each relationship helped me to evolve and be ready for the next person who stepped into my life.

However, there are times we don't understand why things happened the way they did. It could be an illness, child abuse or the death of someone way too young or unexpectedly. Some of these answers may never be revealed to us while we are here on Earth, but people have prevailed over these tragedies and have found ways to triumph over their sorrows. Some people rise up and help others rise. Maya

Angelou and Oprah are two amazing examples of women who rose up to greatness out of seemingly hopeless situations and heartbreaks.

The Universe can send us some tough lessons, but I do not believe in a cruel Universe that would be so harsh as to have someone suffer serious abuse and trauma to an innocent child to understand a lesson. I wanted to remain authentic in my work, so as a believer that everything happens as it should, I had to understand why children suffer. I asked God, the Universe for help, and I was given the answer later that evening.

The Universe is always trying to guide us on our path, and we understand this through lessons, but there is also free will. We can choose at any time to deviate from our path with free will, which many people who are not aligned with truth do every day. People who commit harmful acts are unhealed, leading dark, unconscious lives. They are acting recklessly and irresponsibly from their wounds out of their free will, and they can cause harm to others. The Universe is always trying to guide them onto the correct path, as the Universe is always trying to help guide you out from that darkness as well. We know they were wounded by someone, someone who passed their wounds onto them. However, at each moment we have a choice to say, "I am not going down that path. I don't want to live this way anymore." At every moment we have the choice to say, "I have the power to change my life and change my story."

The more aligned we are on our path to love and the truth, the more open we are to seeing the guidance, and understanding why everything happened as it did as the next step in our journey. Everything starts making sense as a whole. Again, it doesn't make what the hurtful person did *right*, but you will have more clarity. When you have more clarity, you understand that the path to freedom is through love, and the path to self-imprisonment and destruction is through fear. You become more acutely aware of when you act from love and your higher self, or more from fear and ego. This is consciousness: being more aware of ourselves and others.

If you are still beating yourself up about how something did not turn out the way you thought it would, trusting the Universe is imperative. This is when you *must* know and trust, that everything is happening as it should. If it did not happen, it was not meant to happen and you are being redirected to something better, if you continue to trust and follow your path.

It could also be that something didn't happen to force you to rise up and face your fear? Instead of giving up so easily. It is always your choice to be a victim of circumstances or the conqueror of them. When you face your fears, it always strengthens you. What follows next, if you are open to it, will be the next step in your evolution. You leveled up.

To wish anything had been different would change all the events that follow. Know that everything in your life prepares you for what's to come. Stay open and trust the process.

You Are Perfect as You Are
You Are Not Your Story

The above statement is the absolute truth. Did you know that? You are perfect, exactly as God created you. What makes you unique is the reason why God put you are here, because the world needed one of you. The only person keeping you from realizing that is *you*. Your limiting beliefs prevent you from seeing how truly amazing you are. No one can make us feel anything we don't already feel is true about ourselves.

If I said, "You suck at your job," but you know you're good at it, my words would have zero emotional impact on you.

You would think, "Girl, what is she talking about? I'm freaking awesome at what I do!" However, if you felt you weren't good at your job, and I said, "You suck at your job," a comment like that could really crush you.

Do not allow someone else's perceptions to define your life. No one's perception of you defines who you are, as they only see you through their filters. Their perception of you, in actuality defines who they are, not you. Know that you, and only you, hold the power to define yourself. How does knowing that change things? How would you choose to define yourself now?

If you still don't believe you are amazing, the Universe tries to remind you every single day, how loved and wonderful you are. But it is you who keeps disconnecting yourself from this source of love and

from the truth. God's definition of you is the only one you need, and that is *know you are loved. You are perfect, just as he created you.*

I repeat, "You are loved and perfect, just as you are."

What happened in the past wasn't meant to define you, but it can be used to help you grow. Each time we walk away from a job, a lover, or a situation that keeps us small and doesn't allow growth, take what it taught you and learn to choose better next time. Every time we took something for granted, we are taught how to appreciate it more next time. These are our lessons of evolution, and you were guided here as your next step. The lessons on these pages are here to help you remove the many layers of untrue beliefs and stories you've been telling yourself for so long. If you quiet your mind and connect with the Universe through meditation and prayer, you can remain aware of this truth—that you are perfect, whole, and complete as you are.

You are loved. You are never alone. God is always present.
Love is always present.

~ ~ ~

Love vs. Fear

True Self (Soul) vs. False Self (Ego)

I've been talking a lot about your higher self and your true self, compared with your false, fear-based egoic-self. If you are new to this path, you may still be wondering, "what exactly does it mean?" I know I didn't have a clue at first. So, I am going to break it down to help you have a better understanding.

Having an awareness of your false fear-based self can help you identify issues that come up in your life. Once you can differentiate between your true self and your egoic-self, you will be able to recognize when you are in ego and how that influences your perception, your judgments, and your actions; versus when you are resonating from your higher true self, which sees love, compassion, unity, and truth.

Both selves are made up of energies. When you are resonating or vibrating from lower egoic energies, you will view the world as a hateful, fearful place, and you will attract and create more lower energy experiences because of it. When you are resonating from your true-self and higher loving energies, you will attract and create more loving experiences into your life. The world you see around you will always match your energy and perception. Whether you believe this or not, you can't deny the evidence of it in your daily life.

When you're having a bad day, more bad things seem to happen. As more bad things compile, your patience wears thin, and you become more reactive than proactive. Being reactive causes a chain of events that would otherwise not have happened if you were able to take a step back and address it from your calmer, centered true self. With practice, you can learn to respond, rather than to react, to situations. You will see how responding instead of reacting dramatically improves your life and your relationships as well. However, there will still be days when you absolutely lose it, and ego will take over. Forgive yourself. Some situations can understandably make you lose it. It's that you don't want to stay stuck there where you are always losing it about everything. This is a practice in becoming more resilient and as you build your resilience you will bounce back faster, and better than before, becoming more resilient each time.

Keep in mind, this is a practice, not perfection. That is what will keep you even more resilient. It's about creating the life you do want, and not living at the effects of it. Let's face it, life is not always going to be pure bliss, no matter how spiritual or evolved you are. Practicing and knowing how and when to use your tools is essential. That's why the tools are there, to gently guide you back. Taking a step back and centering ourselves through mindfulness, meditation, and awareness allows us to see the situation from a higher perspective. Ego hates taking responsibility, while your soul thrives on it. When you choose to return to a love-based mentality, you see with more awareness and understanding. Thus, you will generate more positive outcomes. Many of us have experienced days when it seems like everything is going right for us. This is when our energy is drawing in more positive people and experiences. We are in alignment with the Universe because we are resonating from our true selves.

Although you're vibrating at a higher level of energy, there may still be times when it seems like we are still attracting unwanted experiences. Pay attention. This can be a test. This is that moment when someone cuts you off on the road, and you have that strong urge to cut them off in return, or when that ex comes back after you've finally gotten over him. Why do these things happen?

This could happen for a couple of reasons:

1) Energetically, the ex can feel you have moved on. This causes them to feel the loss and reach out to you. It does not mean they love you, it only means they want to fill that void with you again.

2) The Universe is testing you to see how much you have learned. Are you going to go back to the ex and give him another chance, losing everything you've gained? However, using everything you learned will push you into the next level. You passed the test.

3) Resistance from ego that things are going good. Ego does not feel safe when things are going well. Ego is always waiting for the next shoe to drop.

Sometimes, these unexpected challenges are something we asked for. In one of her 21-day guided meditations with Deepak Chopra, Oprah said that one year, she asked the Universe to give her "strength." Following that request, one bad thing happen after another. She said that was the last time she ever asked for strength again. The Universe will always send you what you ask for, it just may not be in the form you expected. So be careful for what you ask for and keep trusting the process.

Discovering the True Self

What is your "true self"? Your true self is comprised of your highest self and your soul. Your soul is you in your purest, most loving form, at your current level of awareness. It is you when you feel kindness, compassion, and empathy. It is you, when you create unity, connectedness, peace, and understanding. It is you when you feel inspired, creative, and alive. It is the part of you that is connected to your highest self, God, the Universe, and source energy. It is the part of you that knows it's still evolving and seeks growth, expansion, and awareness.

I remember in the early days of my spiritual practice, I had completed Gabby Bernstein's six-week, "May Cause Miracles" workshop at Integral Yoga in Greenwich Village in New York City, and then enrolled in her four-week, "Fearless Relationships" workshop at Golden Bridge yoga studio in Soho where she told the class to, "Set your intentions to your highest self. We are always praying to our highest selves for the highest good of all."

I remember thinking, "What is she talking about? I don't want to pray to my highest self for the highest good of all. I don't even know what my highest self exactly means? Can't I just pray to meet my new soulmate? That's what I came here for." Even though I knew I was filling a void now that my divorce was over rather than face the inner work, but I didn't care. I just wanted to feel good again.

And it was as if she read my mind, Gabby looked straight at me and said, "Trust me. Just do it." So, I trusted her and went home and started praying to my highest self for the highest good of all. I was still not exactly sure what it meant or what I was doing? In time, I

started feeling a shift in me, and it was amazing. I began to have a new level of awareness. Setting your intentions to reach your highest self and praying for the highest good for everyone works like an umbrella intention and prayer. It covers everything in your life. Usually when we pray, we pray for ourselves, but the Universe loves us all equally. It doesn't want you to beat out Jane; it loves Jane too. So when you pray for the highest good of all, you are praying for the best possible outcome for everyone's well-being and surprisingly, this is the outcome and the happiness you didn't know you wanted. The Universe loves that, and it will create more loving cohesive experiences for you. If you only have one prayer or intention may it be, "Thank you, God, for everything in my life. I pray to my highest self for the highest good of all." You really don't need any other prayer or intention.

When you pray to your highest self for the highest good of all, you start seeing life from a higher perspective with wisdom, love, and understanding. Your entire world shifts. Then, I started seeing everybody in two forms—their wounded egoic false self and their true self. This helped me to see them with more love and understanding. It wasn't what I expected to get out of Gabby's workshop, but this meant more to me than manifesting any soulmate, because it was what I needed for the next step in my evolution. Gabby calls herself the "can opener," and she was breaking me open even further. I was now opened to the expansive love the Universe has for all of us. As I continued onto Gabby's Masterclass Levels One and Two, I began to understand that my awakening was not just about me, my healing, my growth, or my happiness, but to also find my calling to help aide in the healing of the world. This was no accident, but part of God, The Universe's, divine plan.

I was now resonating more from my true self and able to see when I was in ego. It felt so freeing, so loving, so inspiring, and so energizing. How did I not know this sooner? It was like some well-kept secret that I believe needs to be taught to every child. I can only imagine how different my life would have been if I had been taught this growing up. But I also know that society is slowly but surely evolving, through mindfulness, meditation and yoga becoming more mainstream and popular now. It's even being taught in schools, hospitals, police departments, and prisons. These are such exciting developments and where real healing starts to occur.

Something happens to you when you enter this practice. As with anything that changes your life, you want to share it with everyone, because it brings so much peace, love, and joy into your life. You want others to have that peace, joy, and love as well. Although you have to be aware of who you share this message with, because not everyone is ready for it. But do start sharing your experiences with those who are open, because as you teach and ignite someone else's light, you will feel the light within you grow even brighter.

The False Self Defined

Our false, egoic-self behaves and acts like a bratty, immature child. It's everything from our lower energies and where we are working on evolving from. Ego likes to make us think we know everything, and we're always right. It's more interested in winning, feeling like the victim, blaming others, and wanting to be understood, than in trying to understand and compromise. Ego is the side of us that puts up walls. Ego shows up to protect us in its reactive style anytime we feel triggered by something or someone. A spiritual practice helps us to build awareness, especially around ego's triggers, because those are the blocks holding us back from the life we want to live, and how fast can we bounce back from those triggers to our love-based, true selves.

True Self/Soul (Love-Based)	False Self/Ego (Fear-Based)
✔ We	✔ Me
✔ Peaceful	✔ Defensive
✔ Understanding	✔ Biased
✔ Collaborates	✔ Competitive
✔ Inclusive	✔ Exclusive
✔ Compassion	✔ Unempathetic
✔ Equal	✔ Hierarchy
✔ We are one	✔ Winners and Losers
✔ Accepts responsibility	✔ Blames
✔ Knows there are different perspectives	✔ Needs to be right
✔ Wants to Learn and grow	✔ Knows everything
✔ Guides/Inspires	✔ Dictates/Orders
✔ Expansive	✔ Contraction
✔ Knows vulnerability is strength	✔ Builds Walls to Protect

Not All Days Will Be Sunshine and Rainbows

When I first entered this path, I had no idea how amazing it would feel to let go of ego and connect to the light. I was flying high, feeling so connected to Source for several months, then all of a sudden. I felt as though I fell into a dark hole. I had no idea what was happening? I was desperately trying to reconnect to the light, but nothing seemed to be working? It was then I discovered, what I was experiencing was known as, the *dark night of the soul.*

Dark night of the soul experiences suck, big time. Literally, they suck all the light and joy out of you as you are going through them. I wonder if it feels darker now, because you know what light and free-dom feel like? You'll wonder what happened to all that beautiful, lov-ing energy that once surrounded you? It can feel like the worst PMS, depression, and a temper tantrum. You can try every single tool, but nothing seems to work. You may even wonder, "Will I ever feel that light and love again?" Do not be alarmed.

This is how negative energy is released through us. We set an intention for something to be released from us, and this how it is released. That part of our ego is dying. Ego does not like to go down without a fight. But I can attest, after having been through several rounds, you will feel so much lighter when you come out the other side. You will also notice something missing. You'll notice that what once used to trigger you, no longer triggers you. You may have less of an interest in proving yourself to anyone or responding in your old ways anymore. It may be different for you, depending on what you asked to be released and your journey.

Congratulations! You have leveled up again! When you spiritually level up, you become more humble. That part of your ego is gone, and your awareness has increased, because that ego filter has been released from you. As you are going through it, simply recognize it for what it is. Acceptance is the best thing to do to ride it out until it passes. Resistance only makes it worse. What also helps is being grateful and saying, "Thank you God, for taking from me what is not serving me." Meditation, yoga, walks in nature, and surrendering will be your best friends until you get through to the other side.

As you know by now, when we are not feeling love, joy or inspira-tion, it means we have disconnected from Source. Some days, it will be easy to connect with Source. We wake up, the sun is shining, we get out of bed, we feel passionate about life, and we are filled with inspiration. Other days, it can take everything you have to get out of bed and face the day. Sometimes, we're aware of what disconnected us. Something or someone may have triggered us, and we are able to reframe, let it go, and see it with love. Sometimes, it's hormones, or we don't know what is going on? You become very sensitive to energy on this path as you become more aware of light and dark energies. Part of the journey is understanding the positive and negative energies. The goal is not to resist the negative energies, but accept them by saying,

"Oh, there you are again," befriend it, and allow it to move through you. Resisting negative energies, suppressing them only causes them to get stronger. Balance your energies to become less reactive to them and stay as closely connected to light as you can in the process.

There was another time when I was just not feeling it, and I was stuck in it for a long period of time. I am not someone who wakes up pissed off, usually something has to happen to piss me off. Yet here I was, waking up every morning pissed off. I tried everything—yoga, meditation, surrendering, releasing, listening to my inspirational books to help shift my mood and mindset, and nothing was working. I still was not feeling right even after using all of the tools that normally help me. I was about to go into therapy, which I highly recommend if you are troubled with something and don't know how to get out of it yourself. Sometimes just talking to a compassionate ear, someone who understands, and listens without judgment, can help you release it. However, I was guided to buy this homeopathic product that helps with moods and hormones, and voilà! I was cured! The anger disappeared. I later learned through a lot of research, it could also be our diet that affects our moods. We are learning so much how the gut has its own brain and gut bacteria can affect our moods too. So, if you are feeling that you are still suffering from depression or anxiety even though you have done the work, follow your inner guidance on whether you need a therapist, or holistic doctor to help you find the root of the issue. We don't want to reach for drugs first, but they do have a place when absolutely necessary and nothing else has worked.

Intuition vs. Fear

Over time, our life experiences can cause us to stop trusting ourselves and our decisions, or maybe you have become so fearful and cautious, you don't trust anyone or anything anymore? This is primarily because you are relying on fearful ego-based thoughts to guide you rather than following your soul. We have to become aware of the difference between real intuition and ego disguising itself as intuition. But how do you know when you are being led by ego or by a higher power? One of the main ways you can determine is by the amount of fear you feel. Have you ever been totally freaked out, suspecting the worst, but everything turned out okay? On the other hand, have you known something was off, but you had no fear around it? That is how intuition works. Intuition is a knowing; you remain calm. You just know. This is the voice inside you that is trying to guide you. You stay grounded instead of freaking out.

You can start connecting to your intuition by sitting quietly and simply placing both hands on your heart. Think about a situation you would like to understand and see more clearly while focusing on your heart. Say to yourself, "I choose to see this with love. I choose to see the truth." Knowing that love will always connect us with the truth. Trust whatever comes to mind. The more you trust your intuition, the stronger it will get.

Meditation is one of the best ways to connect to your intuition. Meditation quiets the mind to allow intuition to come through. Start by focusing on the space between your eyebrows, known as the third-eye or your center of intuition. You can also connect through the top of your head, your crown chakra, which is our connection to inspiration, Source, and enlightenment.

Sit in easy pose with your legs crossed on the floor, palms facing up, fingertips in Gyan Mudra, with your pointer finger touching your thumb, locking in the energy. The thumb represents our ego, our human form, and our index finger represents our higher self. Then, focus on your crown chakra. Send your thoughts up as high as they can go, until they feel they have connected with divine Source. Then, send your thoughts way down below, grounding you and connecting you to mother Earth. Sit quietly for 2 to 3 minutes, at first. You will increase your time as you become more accustomed and comfortable with the practice. Twenty minutes is usually the standard minimum. With consistent meditation and trusting your intuition, you will see where it is guiding you, and it will become second nature.

Intuition and distinguishing your true self from your ego self, is an integral part of self-awareness, allowing for forgiveness and self-compassion to come through. You will begin to know who you really are and trust your own inner guidance.

~ ~ ~

Self-Forgiveness and Self-Compassion Exercises

It's time to really start trusting yourself and receiving guidance from your intuition rather than your ego and fears. This should be a part of your daily, lifelong practice.

Affirmation: *"I love and forgive myself."*

Song: "Try" by Colbie Caillat

Pocket reminder: Your pocket reminder can be a note with the word "Compassion" or the affirmation, "I love and forgive myself. Today, I will treat myself as my own best friend." It is a reminder to help you stay on your path and show up for yourself every day.

Self-Forgiveness/Self-Compassion Altar Prep

This week, set up your altar with words and symbols on forgiving yourself and self-compassion.

Using Music to Help You Shift or Release Negative Energy

Music is a great tool. Sometimes it can be difficult to move stuck energy. Stuck energy can weigh you down. You can feel angry, sad or *blah* for no reason at all. It could be due to the transition of being single again after a break-up, or sometimes you're not sure why? I don't typically recommend sitting around and listening to music that makes you cry, because many songs without you realizing it can throw you down the emotional rabbit hole and make things worse. If you haven't noticed, you will now.

"Love songs" and I used the word loosely; are particularly guilty of this. These songs are usually about how someone did you wrong, and you were the fool; or they're about unrequited love, with someone saying "I can't live without you." They keep us in a depressive state. It makes us confused because we believe that's what love really is. They should be called "songs to keep me depressed, heartbroken, and stuck in unhealthy relationships." Just because these songs resonate with you doesn't mean it's healthy for your mental well-being. Why do you think they use music in movies? Because they have the ability to control how we feel.

I make sure to stay clear of songs that bring me down, especially when I am already down.

I do, however, highly recommend songs that help you heal when you are feeling down. I sometimes use it as a meditation to release heavy emotions. There's a difference. Listening to songs that heal, like "Let it Be" by the Beatles, or ones that resonate with you help to release that painful stuck energy inside you. Tears may be streaming down my face, but so is the pain and stories I've been holding onto along with it. I feel so much lighter afterwards. That's the difference between songs that heal and songs that keep you down: One sets you free, the other keeps you stuck in the story. Notice how the music you listen to affects you, and use healing music as a tool to help release heavy stuck energy and set you free.

Day 1: Self-Forgiveness and Self-Compassion Exercise

Affirmation: *"I am willing to release old stories about myself that are simply not true."*

Divide a blank sheet of paper length-wise into three columns. In the first column, write the heading "Old Stories." These are the stories you keep telling yourself that are not serving you and are keeping you blocked. Then, select and answer from the questions below. Write your answers into the first column. Follow your intuition and add any of your own questions that apply to you. Leave the other two columns blank until tomorrow.

Self-forgiveness questions:

- What are the false stories and limiting beliefs have you been telling yourself about relationships? (Like, *I'll never meet the right one. I will get hurt. All men are jerks. What great guy could ever love me?*)
- In what ways are you being too hard on yourself when it comes to relationships?
- What other ways are you being too hard on yourself in terms of weight, looks, personality, money, and career?
- What stories have you been telling yourself that are making you feel bad and are lowering your self-worth?

Write down a list of everything you need to forgive yourself for.

If you don't know what your stories are, it's okay. Try setting an intention and ask for it to be revealed to you. Be still and wait for the answer to come. This might take a few days. Get really deep with this question. See what's coming up for you? Keep an eye out for how it's showing up in your present life. The Universe has a way of making you face what you haven't wanted to face, once you set the intention. Notice any patterns? Once we acknowledge our patterns, we can begin to heal them and be free from them.

Altar

Meditation • Prayer • Intentions

Bring to your awareness the ways you have been hard and unforgiving to yourself and how it has been affecting you and your life. Don't judge yourself. Just be a witness to it. Sit in meditation for 5 - 20 minutes. Remember, we can't heal what we won't recognize. Set the intention to bring more awareness to this to clear this from you.

Day 2: Self-Forgiveness and Self-Compassion Exercise

Affirmation: *"I am willing to forgive myself."*

Self-forgiveness exercise:

Today, you're going to write in the second column. At the top of this column write,

"I forgive myself." Answer the healing questions below and write your answers down next to each old story and belief in column 1. Leave the last column blank for tomorrow. If you don't have answers for all the questions, it's okay leave them blank. Answer what you can.

Self-forgiveness questions:

Based on what you wrote yesterday, write down why you are choosing to forgive yourself for this belief or story.

- How is this belief not serving you?
- In what ways is it holding you back?
- How will forgiving yourself for it change your life? How will it feel?

Write down anything else that comes up for you.

Altar

Meditation ▪ Prayer ▪ Intentions

After you complete the exercise, sit in silent meditation on anything that comes up for you that you want to sit with and observe in quiet contemplation, or you can use the bonus gift meditation I created for you on self-forgiveness and self-compassion on my website at:

karenOM.com/resilient-love-meditations
Password: resilientlover

Set an intention: "God, Universe please help me witness and forgive myself for thoughts that do not serve me."

You can write down your intention on a piece of paper and place it on the altar, if you wish (optional).

Day 3: Self-Forgiveness and Self-Compassion Exercise

Affirmation: *"I am willing to see things differently. I am willing to see myself with love."*

Self-forgiveness exercise:

Today, in the third column write down the heading, "My New Story." Answer the questions below and write your answers down next to the second column. Keep this list as a reminder of your self-forgiveness journey and refer to it as needed.

Self-forgiveness questions:

- How can you reframe this story or belief to a positive or compassionate story that works for you, rather than against you?
- How will seeing the story for what it is, and releasing it, help you to have more happiness, freedom, and more of what you do want in life?

If you have a difficult time with these questions, again ask God, your higher self, or the Universe to help you see it more clearly. "Please God, help me to release these stories that are not serving me and help me to see myself through the lens of love in which you see me. Please help me to create new stories that do serve me."

Trust that an answer will be given to you and leave yourself open to receiving it.

Altar

Meditation ▪ Prayer ▪ Intentions

After completing the exercise, sit in silent meditation on today's questions or feel free to use the free mediation on self-forgiveness and self-compassion available on my website, listed on Day 2 exercises.

Set an intention, such as, "Please help me to see myself with love." You may also set your intention or affirmation and place it on the altar (optional).

Day 4

Affirmation: *"I am not my thoughts."*

Self-Compassion Observation:

Throughout the day, pay close attention to how your thoughts are affecting your feelings. When you are having a good day, notice what your thoughts are around that day. Write these good feeling thoughts down as a reminder of your empowering thoughts. Pay attention when you are feeling down. Notice again what thoughts you are having and how they are affecting your mood and your perception.

Write about what you witnessed throughout the day and answer the questions below.

Self-compassion Exercise:

Journal or observe your thoughts on the following:

Write down your observations when you noticed yourself having compassionate thoughts vs. thoughts that did not serve you. How did they affect your mood, actions, and perception differently?

Witness the ways in which ego is showing up. Keep notes and pay attention to how many times you have a disempowering thought that is not serving your best interest or your highest good.

It's perfectly normal to shift from one perception to another throughout the day. This is a good time to get yourself in the habit of forgiving yourself for having a negative or disempowering thought.

Altar

Meditation • Prayer • Intentions

After completing the exercise, sit in meditation on what you observed today or sit in silence, letting go of all the thoughts from the day and opening to receive intuitively. Start becoming aware of what type of meditations work best for you for each situation, if you haven't done so already.

You can set an intention or use an affirmation such as, "I forgive myself for having these thoughts. I always have the choice to choose again." Set your intention or affirmation in writing and place it on the altar if you wish (optional).

Day 5: Self-Compassion Exercise: Journal or Self-Observation

Affirmation: *"Today, I will be kinder to myself and start treating myself as my own best friend."*

It's time to start treating yourself as you would your own best friend. Continue being the observer of your thoughts throughout the week. This time, when you have a self-defeating thought, forgive yourself and use the affirmation or mantra, "Today, I am going to treat myself as I would my own best friend."

Affirmations help to reframe. Mantras are more like your mission statement. Start getting into the habit of catching a disempowering thought, and not judging it. Forgive it and replace it with an empowering thought that works for you.

This will eventually become more natural for you with practice. Jot down any observations.

Self-compassion questions:

- How has being kinder to yourself with compassionate self-talk made a difference in how you feel?
- How does compassionate self-talk change your perception about a situation?
- What shifts are you noticing in your life with self-compassion?
- What are some ways you can be kinder and more compassionate to yourself in order to keep it an ongoing practice?

Remember, you're exercising and building your muscles. The more you practice, the stronger it will become over time.

Altar

Meditation ▪ Prayer ▪ Intentions

After completing the exercise, sit in silent meditation on feeling kinder and more compassionate to yourself, or use music that makes you feel kinder and more loving to yourself; music that makes you feel like being your own best friend. Set an intention or use the affirmation, "I treat myself as I would my own best friend," as your intention.

You may also set your intention or affirmation in writing and place it on the altar (optional).

~ ~ ~

Day 6: Self-Compassion Exercise: Journal or Self-Observation

Affirmation: *"What happened does not define me. I am not broken. I have forgiven myself from the past. I am healing and growing wiser and stronger every day."*

Continue being the observer of your thoughts and using your tools to stay connected to the truth of who you really are. Ask yourself every day, "What is the best thing I can do for myself today?"

Self-compassion questions:

- What was the best thing you did for yourself this week?
- How are you proud of yourself for staying committed to yourself and this practice?
- How are your new stories and beliefs working for you?
- What is the best thing you can do for yourself moving forward?

Altar

Meditation ▪ Prayer ▪ Intentions

After completing the exercise, sit in meditation on your growth so far. You may also sit in silent mediation, letting the day go and clearing the way for something new to come through. You might use a guided meditation from YouTube that is aligned with this exercise. Set an intention or use an affirmation such as, "I always treat myself and others with compassion."

You may also set your intention or affirmation in writing and place it on the altar (optional).

Day 7: Reflection

You made it to the end of week three! Seriously, you should be so proud of yourself for showing up and doing this healing work. These first three lessons are the hardest. I promise you. It will get easier and even fun as you go along. You will feel freer and lighter, if you're not feeling it already.

On the seventh day of each lesson, you will reflect over the week, noting what tools worked best for you. Then, start building your own practice and rituals. This is the hard part. You are doing the work here. After this, keep your practice simple. You are more likely to stay with a consistent, regular practice that is easy and enjoyable.

Bonus exercise: Take the first column, rip it off, tear it up, and flush or burn it. It is no longer you. You can also write out the very thing you are having resistance against. Forgive yourself for having this resistance and set the intention to have the willingness to let it go and allow it to be released from you. Some people choose to save their writings to reflect on in a few months or a year later to see how much they have grown. You'll be amazed!

PART ONE

Self-Love, Self-Care &
Being Wholeheartedly Single

Self-love is the foundation from which
everything else stems from in your life

Self-Love:
What Is It and What It Isn't.
And Why It Is so Important to Love Yourself.

We're hearing a lot of buzz about self-love (and self-care) these days. These are not just buzzwords, nor should they be considered just a trend, but a way of life. Just as much as we place importance on our physical wellness, we need to be emotionally and spiritually fit as well for our optimal mental well-being.

What Self-Love Is and What It Isn't

Despite popular belief, self-love (or "self-care") is not bubble baths, mani-pedis, retail therapy, or a girls' night out, though it may include those things. Self-love is so much more than doing things that make you feel good and pampered to distract you from what's going on in your life.

Other people may confuse self-love with being self-centered and egotistical. Actually, arrogance is the opposite of self-love. Thinking that you're better than someone comes from a place of insecurity, not well-being. It's a self-defense mechanism from someone who is afraid they are not good enough. They puff up themselves in order to feel better about themselves and to protect them from being judged.

"Confidence isn't walking into a room knowing you're better than everyone. It's walking into a room and not feeling like you have to compare yourself at all."
~ Unknown

Arrogance may also be exhibited by someone who was taught to toughen up and not get too emotional. They see vulnerability as a weakness, which is why so many people who believe this to be true suffer silently from depression and resort to handling their emotions through anger, drugs, or alcohol as a way to manage their emotions. Vulnerability and understanding your emotions are actually your biggest strengths, especially in a world that views it as a weakness. Not being able to face your emotions creates weakness. Seeing our vulnerabilities as a gift gives us the ability to strengthen ourselves from our core.

What Is Self-Love?

Pretty much everything you've been working on here—the forgiveness, not holding onto anger or resentment, releasing, letting go, the self-acceptance, loving yourself as you are, self-compassion, your commitment to yourself, and keeping yourself mentally and spiritually fit—are all acts and the crux of self-love. It's knowing you are enough and feeling fulfilled from within. It's healing your wounds and not being the victim, so you no longer suffer from your wounds, but learn how to grow and become empowered from them. It's being kind and compassionate to yourself and others. It's understanding your triggers, so you don't bleed them all over yourself and others. It's liking who you are. Feeling good about being you. It's not conforming to fit in or to be liked. It's honoring and respecting ourselves first, knowing that so much stems from how we feel about ourselves first.

Self-love is being mindful of your inner talk and not beating yourself up, focusing more on the qualities that do make you feel good about yourself. It's being your own best friend and celebrating you when you've achieved something you've always wanted. Why not? Who's better to celebrate you, than you? That's the real love you are giving yourself. Love form the core, from the inside out. The spa days, make-up, and retail therapy are all externals; true love is never about the externals, those are bonuses. And the more you do this work, the less you'll need them to fulfill you. Self-love is staying connected to the light within you, knowing the Universe loves you unconditionally.

Self-love is:

✓ Saying "yes" to more things that feed your soul.
✓ Saying "no" to things that don't.
✓ Facing your biggest fears and getting out of your way, to get more of what you want and deserve out of life.
✓ Taking risks and growing from rejection instead of being defined by it.
✓ Knowing when you need to take time out for self-care.
✓ Seeing through and owning your shit.
✓ Loving and accepting yourself as you are.
✓ Knowing you are enough.

Self-love is NOT:

✓ Thinking you are better than others.
✓ Needing the approval of others.
✓ Allowing the judgment of others to define your worth or dim your light.
✓ About judging others. A great sign that we are not in alignment of loving ourselves is when we are judging others. We are passing our discomfort and placing it onto someone else.

Self-love is knowing that external aspects, like how you look or what you have, do not define you, nor will they bring you true happiness.

Self-love is knowing who you are, what you stand for, and what lights up your soul and enriches your life.

Self-love is not feeling beautiful from the outside but feeling beautiful from within and allowing the beauty of that light to shine through.

Self-love is taking time out for self-care, because you know you can't pour from an empty cup. It's giving yourself a time-out to recharge yourself, so you don't take negative energy out on others. Self-care is taking 20 minutes out for yourself to be alone to meditate or take a walk so you can reset your mind and come back feeling more centered. This is so important for moms, especially if you have a demanding job and your energy is drained. It's better to take that time out if and when you can and come back re-centered, than it is to spend more time with kids being stressed out and reactive. When you're overworked to the point where you're short-tempered, you're not good for anyone. This is why self-care is crucial to a self-love practice.

Self-love is respecting yourself. It's knowing your value and self-worth and removing yourself from situations where you are not being respected or serving your highest good.

Self-love is protecting your energy from negative people who drain or harm you. We can become very sensitive to negative energy on a spiritual path. Over time, as you strengthen your practice, you won't take on other people's energies as easily. You will stand rooted in your light. There is no need to run away from every challenge or discomfort to protect your energy. When you run from everything that drains your energy, you will only become more sensitive to it instead of more resilient to it. However, that doesn't mean you should stay in or expose yourself to negative situations to become stronger.

Self-love is also knowing when it's time to remove yourself from something that is not serving you well. Always find the balance in every situation.

Self-love is sharing truth and light. Sharing truth and light connects us to truth and light.

Self-love is seeing people in their truth and light; this helps us stay connected to our truth and light.

Self-love is knowing you are worthy of receiving this love, even from yourself.

Self-love is being committed to caring for yourself—mind, body, and spirit, and having a daily practice that keeps you inspired and feeds your soul.

Self-love is your relationship with yourself. It is the single most important gift we can give ourselves that builds a healthy foundation from within. How we perceive ourselves and how we think other people view us are direct results of how we feel about ourselves, especially with our romantic partners. When we have a poor image of ourselves, we think we are not worthy of love. We need constant validation to reassure us we are worthy, or we are more attracted to earning someone's love to feel worthy, so you chase the person who doesn't love you to prove your worth, while running away from the one who does love you. Or you may think someone doesn't love you, when they actually do, but ego's need for constant validation has tricked you into believing they don't.

What old story are you repeating to yourself that says you are unlovable and not worthy of love that are simply not true?

The more we love and accept ourselves for who we are, the less we need other people to validate our self-worth. Other people's opinions about you have nothing to do with who you really are. What is important, and what serves you better, is what you think about yourself. The key to being at peace with yourself is applying self-love and self-acceptance.

Self-love is freeing, because it releases us from our self-condemning behaviors, such as being controlled by other people's perceptions and expectations of us. Self-love also makes us genuinely resilient as opposed to the mask of strength, which causes us to "toughen up" and cry behind closed doors; or worse, when you didn't allow yourself to feel at all. Resilience through self-love gives you the inner strength and flexibility to keep going, try again and stop taking things so personally or being so hard on yourself.

Self-Love Is Allowing Yourself to Feel

This may seem repetitive since we just went over the importance of our feelings in our lesson on self-forgiveness. However, I am reiterating it here, because self-love is making sure you put what you've learned into action. This is not about knowledge. This is about building a practice. Life is where you apply it. That is where you will gain the most benefits and freedom.

The belief that you have to toughen up, handle it by yourself, and avoid your feelings leads us down a rabbit hole of despair and self-destructive behavior. When we don't allow ourselves to feel our feelings, we become resistant to who we naturally are, as living, breathing feeling human beings. When we deny what we are feeling, we are also blocking the pathway from Source that nourishes and feeds our soul. Our feelings are there for a reason, because they are signals that reveal essential information about our overall emotional health. Our intuition is like our internal GPS system, and our feelings are like meters telling us what's going on internally.

Anger is a signal telling us maybe a value has been crossed. Jealousy is a signal that tells us our self-worth feels threatened. It doesn't matter if the emotions are true or false; they tell us what we need to address, such as if a partner oversteps a boundary or a wound that still needs healing. When we don't deal with our emotions, because we don't want to feel what has been triggered, they don't go away simply because we chose to ignore them. It's like ignoring the "check engine" light in your car. Ignore it all you want, but at some point, you are going to have to deal with it. By that time, it's usually critical, and it would have cost you a lot less had you taken care of it right away.

Many people escape their emotions through a means called "numbing." That's when they use a variety of coping mechanisms to help them run away from what they are feeling, such as the use of drugs, alcohol, sex, dating, shopping, overworking, overeating, and over-exercising. Even extreme sports are all numbing tools. The purpose of these coping methods is to avoid painful feelings and memories or fill the emptiness they feel inside. But there is really no escape. Instead, it becomes an endless cycle of addiction.

When addiction is taken too far or to the extreme, many people hit *rock bottom*. Rock bottom can be a wake-up call to seek healing. As J.K. Rowling said, "Rock bottom became the solid foundation on which I rebuilt my life." The only way out is recognizing and believing there is way out.

This subject may seem a little dark for a lesson entitled, "Self-Love," but it's a necessary component in understanding why a self-love practice (loving and accepting yourself as you are while learning from your triggers and emotions) is so essential. A 911 self-love practice is critical for someone who has hit rock bottom, since numbing really did nothing to help. Numbing is avoiding your healing, thus not allowing who you really are to come through. People who are numbing are living completely from a fear-based state of mind. What they are seeking is something to save them, when that something *is* them. What they are looking for everywhere is the light which is already inside of them.

Ask anyone who has healed, and they will tell you they found the answers were inside them all along. They learned how to access the light within them. Just hearing that can activate the light within you, too.

This is why we feel disconnected from ourselves when we take part in numbing activities, because they disconnect us even further from who we really are, our soul self. Numbing is when you have allowed ego, the unmanaged wounded child within, to take full reign over how to make yourself feel better, which is why you feel like crap afterwards. When you take part in activities that feed your soul, you never feel empty or regretful; instead, you feel light, energized, and inspired. Taking part in soul-fulfilling activities is what will keep you resilient.

I can't think of a day where I don't say, "I am so grateful for this practice." When I am down, I turn to my practice. When I am happy, I celebrate and give thanks to this practice.

Self-Love Is Allowing
Yourself to Be Loved

Everyone wants to feel loved. It's in our human nature. It is why we are here—to love and be loved. That is our purpose. Some of the most loving, kind, beautiful, and generous souls I know do not love themselves. I did not personally come to this conclusion; rather, when I told people I was writing a book on relationships and self-love, they bravely and honestly told me, "I don't think I love myself." What I did notice is they are smart, beautiful, talented, and successful by society's standards, yet they are still do not love themselves, nor are they truly happy within.

Society says that to be happy, you must have the money, the house, the high-paying jobs, the clothes, the hair, the car, the relationship, etc. The problem with this is that when people get all this *stuff*, many find they are still unhappy. They eventually learn all that stuff doesn't make you happy. Happiness comes from within and is ignited through a consistent and real self-love practice. A good place to start is to free yourself from the conditioning of society's standards and continue working on healing those voids, remembering that you are already whole, complete, and perfect as you are.

What I also noticed about these beautiful friends who said they do not love themselves is that they do not allow themselves to be loved either. I don't mean the kind of love from another that comes from having a great vent session with a friend over a glass of wine about how much life sucks. Then, you have the ugly cry, hug and kiss each other, and say, "I love you," at the end. I'm not criticizing bonding. Connection and bonding are hugely important for us humans, but it goes deeper than that.

We have to be aware of when connection with others is a release and when it gets us further stuck in our stories. Not being aware of this distinction can create a problem. Do you feel better only for the moment, or do you feel healed? With healing, we level up, and we feel better over time. With venting, it becomes a habit, we get stuck in the story, and wind up creating a life we can't tolerate anymore.

What I noticed about people who said they didn't love themselves, is that they have a hard time accepting and receiving love.

In Gary Chapman's book *5 Love Languages*, he outlines the five behaviors people use to love and feel loved, which are: Gifts, quality time, words of affirmations, acts of service, and physical touch. People who struggle with receiving love may be unable to accept compliments. They do not like gifts. They can be very generous and helpful in serving you, but they will not allow anyone to serve them. They love the chase at the beginning of a relationship but grow distant or pull away as the relationship progresses.

If you try to learn more about these people, many of them will turn the focus and attention back onto you, because it's easier for them to love you than to be loved. They may feel they are not worthy of love or attention, or they do not want you to see them as they think they really are. They are the givers. Giving makes them feel the exchange of love, but also keeps people at a safe distance. Receiving love makes them feel too weak and vulnerable. Givers often feel depleted and resentful from giving so much of themselves. Givers find themselves in relationships with takers, because in the beginning, it felt so good to feel needed and loved. Then, as the relationship progresses, they become angry for always having to be the one to give, save, and rescue. However, try to give a giver any love back, and they will often reject it.

Givers often hate to be takers themselves, because the underlying subconscious message is, "I am not loveable or worthy of love." Healing can begin the moment you become aware of this, where the story began, and how to change it to allow yourself to feel safe and to be loved in return. You can begin telling yourself, "It is safe to be loved. I am worthy of love."

Feeling depleted is a good indication of where you are not allowing yourself to receive love in exchange. When you feel depleted, your soul is telling you that you are out of balance in the exchange between you and a partner, a friend, or even yourself.

Givers will complain they're so tired of giving to people who don't appreciate it.

1) Learn to set your boundaries. Stop always giving and conditioning people to be takers from you. Stop setting yourself and your loved ones up for no-win situations. You do something for them, then resent them for it. You feel guilty *not* doing

something for them then resent yourself. Learn to start saying "no," and feel good for honoring yourself and recognizing your limits.

2) Allow your loved ones to give back. Nothing is worse than a partner or a friend who won't allow you to do anything in return for them. Take baby steps and start getting into the habit of allowing yourself to receive. Allowing yourself to receive shows the Universe that you are worthy of it.

In order to have the love we want, we must allow ourselves to be loved and know we are worthy of love. When we want the love we want, again, we must love ourselves first. When we don't love ourselves, we won't believe that anyone else can love us either. When we don't love ourselves we will also keep choosing partners who do not love us either. When we feel unworthy of love, we stop the flow of love, but at the same time, long for it. To minimize our perceived need of love, we may form a hatred for love, stop believing in it or give up on it. If any of this resonates with you and you want to begin to start allowing love to flow into your life, recognize when and how you are stopping the flow of love and start practicing and allowing the flow of love into your life. You can begin by accepting compliments and allowing people to love you and do things for you. Start allowing yourself to be loved.

When you have a healthy self-love practice, knowing you are worthy of love and allowing yourself to receive love, amazing things happen. You stop doing too much for others, and you actually get more back. When you send that message out to the Universe that you are worthy of love, you will receive more love. Be open to it and be so grateful and the Universe will keep sending it to you.

Loving Yourself as You Are

If you are feeling unhappy with yourself right now, it's because you are not aligned with your soul and true nature. Your work is to get yourself back into alignment with who you truly are and as God and the Universe created you and sees you.

You now know that you are not your past or what happened to you, all that is in the past. Every day is a new day to start all over again. Grow from the experience and define who you truly are and who you want to be.

You are not your self-defeating thoughts or what others think of you. What they think about you is a reflection of them. You may feel different and not fit in with some people, and that's okay. They are not your people. The more you accept this and love yourself as you are, as God created you, your confidence will build and the right people who are meant to be in your life will be in your life.

Take a moment to close your eyes and connect to that love and light within you, breathe into this space. Feel that light and love growing bigger and brighter with each breath. Can you feel it? All that loving, beautiful energy radiating inside of you, that, my love, is who you really are. And it is here for you to connect to, whenever you need it.

Loving Our Face and Bodies

I can't write a lesson on self-love without discussing body image and the definition of beauty in our culture. This issue affects the self-worth and self-image of millions of women around the world, especially here in the U.S. —in places like New York and L.A. —where the standard is set for fashion and beauty. We have been raised in a society where the media dictates how we should look. These standards are so impossible that even the models can't live up to the criteria without their photos being edited to create this fantasy.

The soap and body-care company, Dove, started a revolution to counteract these impossible beauty standards placed on women with its "Real Beauty" campaign. Using time-lapse technology, they showed a model without make up and the team of experts (including makeup artists, hair stylists, and photo editing) it took to make her "beautiful."

Dove continued to revolutionize popular culture by replacing models with real women's body images in their campaign. While women loved the new body image representations, it took other companies ten years to follow suit. The false image of perfection was so ingrained in our society, it became the norm for measuring a woman's "beauty." With the massive increase of positive body messages, Target and CVS have joined the movement by using real life body images. Target is using a variety of body images in their women's swimsuit campaigns, and both Target and CVS are using the representation of real and natural beauty in their cosmetic campaigns, without the use of Photoshop. Going one step further, online clothing store, Asos, did not remove a model's stretch marks from the images in the release of their summer lines. What this movement is saying is, "Yes! We are humans, and we are finally allowed to be humans! And we are beautiful as we are!" What a beautiful thing it is when natural is more beautiful than fake.

Models and celebrities have been speaking out about this for a long time, letting the public know they do not look like their publicized images. Actress Kate Winslet and singer Lady Gaga have both publicly spoken out against magazines that distorted their bodies with Photoshop. Singer Alicia Keys stopped wearing makeup altogether, even at the Grammy Awards. People either think she is weird or brave. Our response to her decision actually reveals how conditioned we are. Even considering this as an act of bravery and not normal says a lot about our society and how superficially conditioned we are. I think Alicia would agree. We have been so conditioned to believe we are unacceptable and not beautiful as we are.

It breaks my heart when I see young women in tears, because they feel they do not measure up to these unrealistic images. They did not grow up in a time before readily available image editing. Now, photo manipulation is as easy as downloading an app. Teen anorexia is at an all-time high, because young girls are being influenced by these images and believe it's important to reach these standards. They haven't matured enough to see how unimportant it really is. They believe what's being fed to them, just as we have.

On YouTube, girls as young as twelve years old talk about their knowledge of beauty creams on what worked and what didn't work to help them look younger. You heard that right, at *twelve years old*. That is a new learned behavior of this generation, because looking younger never entered our minds when my friends and I were twelve. All we cared about was designing our denim loose-leaf binder with cool stickers and flavored lip gloss. When I saw what was happening with these young women; helping women love themselves as they are; helping them believe they are beautiful as they are, became another passionate mission of mine.

We have more power and a stronger voice than we realize. It's not up to the magazines, movies, TV, Instagram, and doll manufacturers to dictate how we should look. As the consumer, we have choices and the buying power to say, "No." This has already led to some toy companies creating more realistic dolls in different ethnicities and body types. Some companies are more forward thinking in their beliefs and mission, while many of the bigger conglomerates will jump on the bandwagon to sell you anything you're willing to buy. I mean take a look at "organic" Doritos.

This is not about "taking down" the fashion and beauty industry or even being against it. I enjoy fashion and make-up. Fashion and beauty are wonderful art forms and an outlet for creative expression of yourself. My message here is about keeping the industry realistic and not letting them dictate to you unrealistic images of who they think you should be.

Sexual Objectification

The sexual objectification of women is a similar issue that is ingrained in our society and media. You might agree or think "It's not that big of a deal. We're all sexual human beings." As a woman, it may make you feel sexually liberated. But using our sexuality to receive validation from men to prove that we are beautiful and worthy; and feeling unhappy when we are not receiving that attention, is another indication that we are using our sexuality to fill voids within ourselves, rather than knowing we are already beautiful, worthy and whole, as we are.

Why is sexual objectification harmful to women? Most women can see men as sexually desirable, and at the same time, as soulful human beings. We are conditioned that way. We're conditioned to dream of love and romance with "the one." However, men have been conditioned by society and the media to believe that women are merely sexual objects, not as sexual human beings, but as "objects" for man's pleasure. There's a huge difference. You may feel flattered to be the

object of a man's desires, but once you truly understand the meaninglessness of being an object, you won't want that kind of attention.

For men who objectify women, who she is, her hopes and dreams are cute hobbies. He's the man. To these guys, women are objects to make them look good, feel good, to keep them happy, satisfied. If you still don't believe this is true, next time you meet a guy who thinks you're so beautiful or hot, keep your eyes open to how much he is really interested in you as a person or is he more fixated on how sexy and beautiful you are "baby?"

So what's the problem you may still be thinking? The problem comes, if the relationship does progress and you want to be included in a major decision, your decision doesn't count. The problem comes when you want to do something for your growth or to pursue your dreams, he has little to no interest. The problem comes when you want to be taken seriously, and you're not. The problem comes when you need him to be there for you, he can't.

If something comes between you and this guy, his needs will always come first. All your dates and your choices will revolve around him. Everything revolves around him. This guy is closely related to the emotionally unavailable guy and the narcissist. You are purely there for his needs and his needs only.

Not all men fall into this category, but it's good to be aware of the signs. Men who objectify are not only "players." Some are the nice traditional guys who think women are second class citizens, just a pretty arm piece, who cooks and cleans for him as well. You may think, "That's just the way men are," or that "men just don't know how to communicate." But that's not true. There are men who do know how to communicate. And there are men out there who are not only respectful of women's opinions, but who value a woman's opinion.

You may think guys who support women's rights are a good bet. But let's say this guy doesn't want a commitment. That's fine, that is his choice. If he's upfront with you that he doesn't want a commitment from the beginning, then he has been respectful of you and has rightfully given you a choice to stay or go. But, if he's not upfront and he keeps you wondering where the relationship is going? Then he doesn't support or respect women like he thinks he does. It's not your fault for not asking him; it is his responsibility to be transparent.

Transparency is respect. And women's rights are about respect. If you are interested in meeting someone to form a committed partnership, you have the right to know whether he wants a relationship with you or not. It is, however, your responsibility to remove yourself from a situation if you want a relationship and he does not. It is also your responsibility to remove yourself if you do not feel safe, secure, or respected. Those are your rights in a relationship. It is not his responsibility to honor those things if he has not done so in the past, but you keep coming back hoping or insisting that he change. However, a man who respects women and himself, will always let a woman know where the relationship is going and let you go if he's not the guy for you. A man who respects women will never leave her feeling confused or unsure about what's going on?

A man who objectifies women, never sees passed her exterior. Through his lust, he may think he's sees into her soul but he never scratches the surface. Unfortunately, it won't be until she loses her beauty, through age, weight gain, child bearing, or illness, and he loses interest or finds another object, that she finds out it was never love. He never really knew who she was or loved her to begin with he was only in lust with her exterior and what it did for him.

~ ~ ~

Imagine for a moment, if we lived in a society that loved us for our inner beauty. And we worked as hard on cultivating our inner beauty as we do on cultivating our outer beauty. Imagine if we only sought partners who loved us for our souls rather than who loved us for our physical beauty. How different would the world be? How would that change everything?

~ ~ ~

Building More Awareness

If you haven't noticed by now, everything in this program is about self-love and building your awareness. I know, I've said it a hundred times. You now know, self-love isn't about pampering yourself and

just reciting affirmations of self-love. It's watching your thoughts and being more compassionate to yourself. It's knowing when you are causing your suffering, calling yourself out on your shit and choosing a more loving response next time. It's knowing when you are acting out of fear or responding from love. It's honoring and respecting and aligning yourself with what you do want in life. These are the practices of self-love that strengthen our abilities and awareness.

Awareness is understanding your triggers and the triggers of others. It's being non-judgmental of yourself and others. Knowing when you are responding instead of reacting. Noticing how everything interacts, reacts, and responds to each other. It's knowing when someone else is acting from a wounded part of their ego or from their true self. What better gift of self-love and compassion than to recognize when someone else is acting out of their wounds? How is that an act of self-love? You will react less to someone else's behavior when you understand they are wounded and get triggered just like you.

When we understand others and forgive, we bring more peace and harmony into our lives and into the world.

Part of a self-love practice is knowing it's doesn't prevent bad things or bad feelings that come up in life, but to help you understand your triggers, so you stop reacting to them. Over time and with practice, you will be less triggered, and more understanding. I can't stress enough, that you will get out, what you put into your practice. However, it is also important to practice with loving passion and not manic obsession. As you continue your journey, you will continue discovering what tools work best for you in different situations. When you're stressed, it may be peaceful silence or guided meditation. When you feel triggered, it may be a run, then maybe an awareness meditation, feeling your emotions and accepting what you are feeling. Try journaling to go deeper to understand what you are feeling and why? Ask for guidance and trust what comes up. Somedays, you may not need to go deep, you just need an affirmation for a good boost.

New spiritual or personal development books are great for a new perspective. Honestly, the messages will always be the same. *Your thoughts are an illusion. Quiet your monkey mind. Be present. Be love. Be kind. Connect to Spirit. Do not judge yourself or others. Forgive.* It's just someone else's take on it that can shine a new perspective on it for you in a different way. Just like this book. Listening or reading books, just like meditation, can also help interrupt and redirect the constant chatter and tape going on in your head and replace it with something good. Although they may not realize it, this is why many people find escape through fictional books or television. It's redirecting their thoughts. However, spiritual books help you to evolve on your journey overtime.

~ ~ ~

If you find yourself clinging onto something too much—a thought that isn't serving you, or waiting for your ex or a friend to call, or clinging to friends to save us. This is a good time to try practicing non-attachment. Become aware of your attachment and practice releasing it. Just the awareness that you are clinging to something can help bring relief.

Forgiveness, letting go and reframing are good tools to use often. The more we learn from our life lessons, we can not only release the pain and suffering, but it also gives us the opportunity to create something new and positive from it. My life could have been very different from where it is now had I not chosen to let go of the past, forgive it, and reframe it into something new that works for me rather than against me. You can't thrive or live the life you dream of having, if you keep holding onto what others did to you.

Every single one of us will experience some type of hurt, pain or rejection at some point in our lives. Rather than running away, hiding from it, and allowing it to define you in a negative way, find the courage to take the risk and build something new out of it. Our purpose in life is to take our pain and transform it into something healing and loving for ourselves and others. This is where you can find hidden gifts inside of you.

With awareness, you know that someone can harm you, but it is your choice to remain a victim of it. You rise above it. You won't continually throw yourself into a downward spiral of negativity and anger and stay there. However, if you do find yourself there, and let's face it, we all do once in a while, you will bounce back faster and better than before. Your self-love practice will center you and remind you of who

you really are. As French philosopher, Teilhard de Chardin is credited to have said, "We are not human beings having a spiritual experience; we are spiritual beings having a human experience."

At this point in time, we are humans living in a world that is just waking up. Today, we are a more conscious society than ever before, which is very exciting. But at the same time, let's face it, the majority of humankind are still pretty unconscious choosing fear. When we finally become a fully conscious, self-aware society where we choose love over fear, we will be able to love and trust freely. This most likely won't happen within our lifetime, since we are still slowly evolving. So, until then, we must learn to love unconditionally, know where to set our boundaries. Identify when we are out of balance and move back into alignment.

I find so many great life metaphors while practicing yoga, such as when I am in a balancing pose. If I focus too much on balancing, I fear I am going to lose my balance, and I will inevitably fall over. If I'm consumed with thoughts from the day and not focusing on my balance at all, I inevitably fall over. However, when I focus lightly on balancing and let go to find my drishti (my focal point), I am able to find my balance. In my daily life when I'm off balance, I know it is because I am out of alignment. I will go back and check how far I have swung the pendulum from fear to love. Once I find the balance, I am aligned again.

~ ~ ~

Self-Care is Self-Love in Action

You've already released a great deal of what has been holding you down, which has allowed you to clean the slate and invite good energy to flow through you. The following action steps are more fun and inspiring than the written self-awareness exercises we did in the last few lessons. And the benefits will be as rewarding. You cannot have one without the other. Work and play bring an appropriate balance to a healthy self-love practice. They go hand in hand.

Remember, we are layering our practice. So, if anything unexpectedly comes up for you, or you feel you are not ready to move forward yet, follow your intuition and go back to Lessons 1 and 2, if you feel called to do so. This is your practice. You will be continuing it long after you complete this program, so be aware of what's best for you, and continue making it your own.

From this day forward, make time to select something from your Self-Care and Self-Love Exercises.

Self-love also means knowing that we always have choices. Not making a choice is *also* a choice. We learn to build our internal foundation with love, wisdom and intuition. When we are connected intuitively to our highest self, we are the most creative and inspired. Trust that you are being guided by the Universe as you allow yourself to be. You and the Universe are one.

Self-Love Assignment: Create a Loving Space

I love giving clients the self-love assignment to fill their home and surround their space with uplifting words, colors, and images that bring them joy the moment they look at them. Phrases such as, "Believe in your dreams, and they will come true;" "See the good in people;" "Believe in miracles;" "Be your own kind of beautiful;" and "Namaste" are some of the beautiful loving words that surround me in my space. Being surrounded by inspiring words and your favorite colors will make you feel good. Seriously, you can't feel bad when you read these words. And if you're having a bad day, they can bring a great deal of comfort. Just go to your local home store, or search on the internet, or be crafty and create your own. If you can't afford to buy a new poster right now, write the words on paper and tape them to your walls and mirrors. You can drastically change your environment and mood at a budget that works for you. It's a fun and easy project.

Self-Love is Self-Care Action Steps

Select one self-care item every day from the list or be creative and come up with your own. Self-care items are things that feed your soul, to reconnect and re-energize you.

- Walking in nature or on the beach.
- Yoga and exercise.
- Meditation.
- Essential oils and aromatherapy.
- Take a bath.
- Cooking: Try a new yummy and nutritious recipe.
- Mani-pedi, haircut, facial or other specialty beauty routines. (Yes, it's on the list, if you're doing everything else).
- Read a book with a cozy cup of tea and comfy PJs.
- Read poetry—love poems by Rumi is a great selection.
- Get plenty of rest.
- Color a mandala coloring book.
- Connect with friends and talk about what inspires you or ways you find healing.
- Set an intention for growth.
- Read books on personal growth that light you up.
- Take a workshop or a new class.
- Do something out of your comfort zone that challenges you.
- Do something fun and new.
- Do something creative.
- Take yourself out to lunch, bring a great book with you.
- Drive on a beautiful open highway with your favorite music blasting loud.
- Add your own...

Principles for Setting a Strong Self-Love Foundation

✔ Showing up for yourself daily—loving yourself so much you make a commitment to yourself and your practice.

✔ Always honoring yourself.

✔ Be kind but saying "no" to what you don't want. Stop people pleasing (always respect and be true to yourself—this is part of honoring yourself).

✔ Being mindful of your thoughts.

✔ Being compassionate to yourself.

✔ Forgiving yourself.

✔ Love, love, love yourself as you are. You are healing, and you are growing!

✔ Protecting your energy and keeping it balanced.

✔ Not judging yourself (or others).

✔ Not comparing yourself to others. Everyone is on their own journey—their journey is not your journey.

✔ Releasing idols (remembering we are all equal).

✔ No need to puff up, you will not find your true strength there.

✔ Set boundaries.

✔ Always accept where you are.

✔ Celebrate your successes.

✔ Surround yourself with people who bring out the best in you and want the best for you. The people who want to see you succeed. Stop trying to prove your worth to people who don't see it.

✔ It's okay to remove people from your life who drain you and don't want the best for you.

✔ Know your voice is as important as anyone else's.

✔ No one is ahead or behind. Everyone is your teacher.

✔ Remember to always reconnect to Source when you are out of alignment

~ ~ ~

Self-Love Means Doing the Inner Work

There is a ton of feel-good, high-vibe information out there, which has an important place for those on a spiritual path who have already done the work, but it's only going to provide a temporary fix if you haven't done the work. Nothing is going to work for you and set you free from your pain unless you do the work. And that means looking at the not-so-pretty parts of ourselves, feeling we are not enough, our self-loathing, our jealousies, anger, what annoys us, what scares us—and facing them head-on, understanding the root cause, and shedding light on them. Sometimes it means embracing our darkness like a small, angry, hurt, frightened child with love and tenderness. What we need is to add more love, not less love to our wounds. You want to make sure you are in a safe loving place to heal it.

Raising your consciousness and expanding your awareness is the key to freeing you from that small frightened child to open yourself to a more peaceful, loving, and happy life. When I first entered this path, I thought it was simply about being positive and high vibe, but as I've grown on this journey, I came to realize everything is about our *awareness of ourselves and* the world, then being high vibe comes naturally. You begin to understand, love, and accept people as they are. You see the beauty and magic of the world around you and instead of the world's weight on your shoulders, you feel the lightness and expansion of the Universe. Transformational work, whether with a coach, a book, or a workshop will continue to help you along this path to have your life changing epiphanies and shifts in your perception a lot sooner than if you sat at home trying to figure it out yourself, avoiding frustrating patterns and repeated lessons. You absolutely need to start trusting in your inner guru, but make sure the inner guru you're listening to is your higher self and not ego. Your inner guru is always trying to show you the next step that will take you to the next level. If you are really open and ready for change, you should already be having massive shifts along the way while reading this book. If you're still having trouble, no worries, and no judgment. Stay open and willing. Fear may still be blocking you somewhere with doubt or resistance. Remember, you always have a choice to choose again. Always.

If you are having trouble shifting, it's important not to judge or blame yourself that you are doing something wrong. One trick is to do a self-love or loving kindness meditation that will help you to shift the blame off you or someone else and see more through the lens of love. When you see through the lens of love, you will be more open and have more shifts. Keep repeating and surrendering as often as necessary until you move through it. It can sometimes take a while, so be patient with yourself.

As you move forward on this path, you will keep layering these lessons and continue to feel your old stories peeling away as you open up to more awareness to a more enlightened and grounded you. As you move forward, go back to some of your favorite old personal growth and spiritual books, (I hope it includes this one), and you will find they may have a deeper meaning for you because you will be in a higher, more elevated space (of love). That's how you know this is truth, because unlike stories that stay the same, spiritual work only gets deeper. You'll find you hear it differently than you did the first time, because when you read it the first time, you were just discovering these new thoughts and ideas and how they pertained to you. Sometimes you go back, and it's like reading it for the first time. That's because we can only see the message when we are ready to receive, which is why this work is so amazing. The deeper we go, the greater revelations we receive. And the more clarity we gain, more is revealed to us.

As you continue on this path, you may also find that things that used to interest you, no longer interest you, like fashion magazines or junk TV. This is perfectly normal. It is because that part of your ego is shedding and no longer resonates with that form of entertainment. You may begin losing interest in going to nightclubs and the party scene and are more interested in spiritual and enlightenment workshops. You will want to spend less time with people who want to talk about lower vibrational activities, such as gossip, comparison, criticism, blame and judgment of other people. Friends and family may distance themselves from you too, because they do not resonate with your new higher loving vibration. This does not make you better than them, you're just in a different space. Some people don't want to do the work as you have done, and they will turn away from you, because looking at you makes them see things they don't believe are possible because ego is still protecting them, and blinding them with fear. Let the things that need to fall away, fall away. Everything you are shedding is revealing who you really are and who you were meant to be, and you will call new people into your life who match this new energy and help you on this path. Trust and believe in the process.

Spiritual Ego

I think it's important that we talk about spiritual ego, so as not to fall into its trap. Spiritual ego can happen when someone enters this path, feels more enlightened; see the changes it's created for them in their life, then thinks it makes them better than others who are not on this path.

I see a lot of spiritual memes on social media that have more to do with spiritual ego than enlightenment. And these come from pages and people who identify themselves as "enlightened" or "conscious." Then they post a meme or a comment that makes them superior to others, such as, "I don't see what people say, I watch what they do" or "spiritual people can always see through fake people," and so many dozens more. And you see all these people "Liking" these posts and comments, misleading others on what being spiritual means.

I know people who are turned off to yoga because they think people who do yoga think they are better than others. You can say, they need to do their inner work, but at the same time, yoga is not about Lululemon, yoga poses, green juice, and thinking you're spiritual. Most of a spiritual practice happens off the mat when you're triggered, and you practice responding from a more grounded heart-centered place. If I am at yoga, I am either there to release and surrender, give thanks, or both. Mostly, both. I'm definitely not there to show off my poses. If you're in my yoga class you know I'm no Instagram yogi! But I love the practice so much, nonetheless. And, I love watching others do well in their practice.

A true Spiritual practice is about about lifting each other up and helping each other rise. It's about understanding, love and compassion, non-judgment. It is never about being superior to another person. The moment you think you are more spiritual than another person, you are out of spiritual alignment. That person who annoys you or you think is less spiritual than you, has just become your teacher. A spiritual practice is not being suspicious and seeing through another person's B.S. and calling them out on it. It's about witnessing your own B.S. and calling yourself out on it. A lot of people have the huge misconception that being spiritual means being super intuitive of funky energy, but many of them are confusing intuition with suspicion. They are receiving from a place of fear and ego, not from spirit. That's the opposite of a spiritual practice or enlightenment. Spirit only sees us with love. They've become out of alignment with spirit. Out of alignment with love. This practice is not about focusing on others except in service to others; a spiritual practice is about focusing inward on yourself. And giving others the space to be on their own journey.

The moment you catch yourself judging others or blaming them that is the moment you redirect your focus off of them and back onto you. And without judgment, take a step back, breathe, and ask yourself, "what is it that is triggering me here? What wounds of my own, am I projecting onto to this person?" If you need to set boundaries, do it in a healthy way. If anything, this practice drops you to your knees and humbles you and makes you more compassionate and understanding of others. A spiritual practice is releasing judgment which comes from a reactive triggered place; however, a spiritual practice does use discernment which comes from thinking things through from a more loving healed place and our higher selves.

A spiritual practice is about aligning ourselves with love and bringing more love, healing, and peace on earth.

~ ~ ~

PART TWO

Becoming Wholeheartedly Single

*"What's missing in your life is not another partner.
What's missing from your life is you"*

What it Means to Be Wholeheartedly Single

Self-love plays a significant role in relationships, bringing us back to our lesson that we must love ourselves first, knowing we are worthy of real love and how our relationships are our assignments. The partners we select mirror back how we feel about ourselves. Our mirror also shows how we are subconsciously attracted to another person's wounds that are as big or bigger than our own. The more we love ourselves, the smaller our wounds will become. Then, we won't need a partner to fill those voids in us, because we are whole and complete within ourselves. We are no longer relying on a partner to make us feel whole. The more we love ourselves, the more we know our value and self-worth in relationships, and the less we tolerate relationships that do us more harm than good. When we know our value and self-worth, we raise the vibration of our experiences and the people we attract into our lives. If you love yourself, you will attract partners who also love themselves and are more genuine and authentic. At the same time, you will lose interest in unhealed partners.

A lot of women who have never been married want to find "the one." I know, I felt this way before I got married. I thought I couldn't be happy without a partner. And when I did get into a relationship, I thought my partner was responsible for making me happy. I really believed we were supposed to make each other happy. I believed that the purpose of a relationship was to fill each other's emptiness and make each other feel whole and complete (I know other people, including men, who believe this too). Because of this, I thought I needed to find a partner in order to be complete. Movies and society condition young women to look for Prince Charming or "the one." Then, friends and family ask single women, "Who are you dating?" "When are you going to get married?" "What's wrong with that guy?" "What are you looking for?" "What are you waiting for?" "Why are you still single?"

Stop!

Today, I realize how much harm those questions and movies do, because they cause women to be ashamed of their singleness and they think being in any relationship is better than being alone and single. Not true.

Then our self-worth becomes attached to our relationship status. In order to detox from this belief, you must first identify when others are imposing their beliefs and judgment onto you. Imagine if a relative thought you should be in an arranged marriage. You would think they were out of their mind. You would probably laugh it off. The same should be if they ask if are you dating someone? It should have no effect on you. The only reason it does is because of your own insecurities about the situation. Don't allow anyone to impose their beliefs onto you. What they are doing is projecting their own insecurities and beliefs onto. They can't be happy without someone, they can't be alone, and they think everyone else needs to too. I had one friend's old-fashioned mother, even though she was in a happy marriage, would tell her daughter when she was single, "Being in a bad relationship is better than not being in a relationship." There was a lot of shame around being single when she was young. Also because women were not in the work force like today, so they were financially dependent on men. This is such harmful advice. The belief that we need to be with someone comes from outdated conditioning. You are not here to make your friends or relatives happy by living your life the way they want, but to lead a life that is right for you and only you. Your worth is absolutely and unequivocally not attached to your relationship status.

Listening to someone else's beliefs over your intuition could lead to a lot of unhappiness for you down the road. It's much better to be alone than in the wrong relationship or to be with someone just to be with someone. You'll know when the time and person is right, until then, enjoy this time. Use it to create something new and wonderful out of it.

~ ~ ~

For centuries and in our not-too-distant history, it was necessary for a woman to have a partner. It was uncommon and unwelcome for a woman to be in the workforce, so she needed a man to financially support her. In turn, she did her part by taking care of the household and the children. In this sense, they completed each other. However, over the years, women fought for their rights to be in the workplace and for equal rights, but the belief that we need partners to complete us still remains and continues. We need to evolve from this theory. A woman most certainly can stand on her own, but we need to separate ourselves from the belief that we are incomplete without a partner.

Today, we have a choice to be in partnerships, because we don't need a partner. We can choose to be in a relationship with a person who enhances our life. You can connect with someone you genuinely like and love for who they are, not your financial need of them. In a wounded relationship, it is not uncommon to be in love with someone you don't like or even respect, but out of your need of them. How crazy does that sound? In a healthy relationship where each partner is a whole individual, you *complement* each other, rather than *complete* each other. You are together because you want to be together, not because you need them. You are not busy trying to fill each other's voids, triggering wounds, and trying to heal from them. Instead, the love is a free-flowing exchange. If you spend less time on drama, you can spend more time on doing great things together, like volunteering, helping the community, working for the greater good of mankind and the planet, than on each other.

I see being single as my "non-dependence" on someone else to make me whole, happy, and complete. I am happy, whole and complete as I am. This is what I call being "wholeheartedly single." This is important, because there are so many women who feel inadequate and ostracized by society, because they don't have a partner and wind up in toxic and dysfunctional relationships. Men have told me they often hear the pressure too. Fear of being single will cause women to put so much work into a painful or dead-end relationship rather than putting that effort into aspiring to their own greatness. If you're going to work on something, instead of working to try to get a boyfriend, try working on yourself and creating your own great story is where your time is better spent. Don't waste it on painful relationships that keep you small and hold you down. Know your worth. Don't let anyone take you away from your own greatness, especially yourself. A partner who is secure and whole within himself will always honor and support your success. Love should be the easiest part of the relationship.

The next time someone asks you, "Why are you single?" you can proudly look them in the eye and say, "I see singleness as my non-dependence on someone else to make me happy and complete" or "I love my life as it is. If I meet the right person, wonderful. I don't need to be *with someone* just to *be with someone*."

You can also say, "You know, there are a lot of unhappily married people out there. I don't want to be in a relationship just to be in a relationship to make other people happy. When the right person comes along, great, but until then, life is pretty awesome as it is. I don't need to define myself through another person. I want someone who complements my beliefs and personality. It may take time to find that person, but it's worth the wait." And if they say, "Can you afford to wait?" Tell them, "I can't afford *not* to wait."

Even when you say this to yourself as your truth, it sends that intention out to the Universe, and it will become your reality.

This may be new to you, and you may still believe you need a partner to complete you. Ego may even have convinced you that your need is actually a want. The quickest way to determine whether you want or need a relationship is to ask yourself if you can do a dating detox for six months. If the thought of that sends chills up your spine, then your *need* is disguising itself as a *want*. This means you need to be in a relationship to feel complete.

You might say, "I'm fine with that need." Then there is a higher probability that somewhere down the road, problems will arise, because you will either choose a partner who isn't emotionally healthy, or you'll be unhappy when your partner stops fulfilling your needs. The purpose of a relationship is not to make you happy or fill your needs. You are responsible for that, not your partner (you should want to be with your partner because you love *them*, period). That's a lot of responsibility to put on someone. After a while, your partner will grow exhausted from having to please you all the time and meet your demands. Healthy relationships have two partners who complement each other's style and love each other for who they are. The more you align with this, the more this person who aligns with you will show up for you.

Start looking around you for the source of your beliefs about relationships. Who taught you that you needed a partner? Was it your family, friends, books, movies, songs, society, or all the above? Once you identify the source, refuse to be influenced by it any longer. The stronger you stick to your non-dependence, the stronger it will become. I choose to say, "non-dependence" rather than "independence," because independence has a connotation of not wanting to partner with anyone. Non-dependence implies your non-dependency of needing someone. The dating detox is a really important step to set yourself free of this conditioning.

Being wholeheartedly single is different from someone who has closed off their heart and no longer believes in love. Someone who has tried many times and can't find someone and has given up on love, or they've closed off their hearts to love, because they're afraid of getting hurt again. To protect themselves, they wear their independence like a shield. What they don't realize is: It's the shield that is keeping them single. If they were brave enough to remove fear and open their heart to love again, they could allow romantic love to flow into their lives again. You may think, "I've tried that, but all I found were losers." That is because your walls are still up; you're on defense mode. You expected losers, so all you see are losers.

You don't go out on date looking to be disappointed or trying to make someone prove themselves to you. Who wants to go out with that? Relax and have fun. Put your armor down. Ask yourself if you are really giving this person a chance? What can you find that you do like about them?

Maybe you're older and think, I'm too old to date again. It doesn't matter how old you are, love is possible at any age. All you have to do is believe.

~ ~ ~

Protecting your heart does not make you strong or resilient in love. It makes you afraid. It may keep all the hurt and pain out, but it also keeps a lot of good things from coming in, like love. I am here to tell you that you are deserving of the type of love you want, but you have to be willing to open your heart and know that you are worthy of that kind of love.

One of the key factors to resilience is staying whole and complete and finding that love within yourself. "Wholeheartedly single" means we love ourselves, and our hearts are open to romantic love. But the purpose for romantic love is not connected with our desire to fill an emptiness within us; rather, we aim for true partnership.

A wholeheartedly single person can take his or her time in finding the right partner who complements them. A wholeheartedly single person does not need hookups, flings, or someone in between to pacify them until they meet the right one, that's the wound. The wholeheartedly single person is already complete within themselves. They are only interested in seeking partners who are whole and complete within themselves. A wholeheartedly single person loves men and does not see them as enemies or other women as competition, but as connected brothers and sisters in this life. As a wholeheartedly single person, we understand the life lessons that come with love, and we use them to keep growing and evolving through our relationships, taking us to the next level. This is what keeps us resilient.

~ ~ ~

Men are Made to be Martians
Women are Made to be Venusians

Men and women behaving like they are from different planets had its place during a different time. Society is becoming aware how much we have been conditioned to play these gender roles. Stereotyping is when we say things like, "You can't do that, because you're a girl, or because you're a boy." It's harmful to our children when we don't encourage them to be all that they can be. We encourage boys to be astronauts and builders, and girls to play with makeup and toy kitchens. Rather than encouraging girls to be scientists and leaders. It's harmful to boys to say, "Don't cry like a girl," when they are hurt. Boys are humans just as girls and need to express their emotions freely, so they don't have to recover from not being able to express their emotions later in life.

Why is non-stereotyping boys and girls so important? Men are taught that it's important to be tough, cool, confident, play the field, get the chicks, make lots of money, drive a fancy car, look cool, act cool, and not show any emotions. They are told from a very young age, "Toughen up, and be a man. Don't act like a girl."

Women are taught their value is tied to how pretty and thin they are and what clothes they wear. They are taught to find that elusive Prince Charming who will save and take care of her. Both men and women have been conditioned that self-worth is tied to what they have, who loves them, and what they look like, rather than who they *are*. A man will find a beautiful woman to share his life with, but a conscious, evolved man will find a beautiful soul-partner to build a life together with.

A conscious, evolved woman knows she can save herself. Not needing a man to fill her needs, she seeks a partner with whom she can create something and contribute to the world together. A conscious partnership has healed their wounds; therefore, they have more time to create and do beautiful things together than unhealed relationships, in which partners spend more time fighting with each other. There is not much room for anything else in the relationship. Great examples of couples we all know who operate like partnerships are Bill and Melinda Gates, Priscilla Chan and Mark Zuckerberg, and

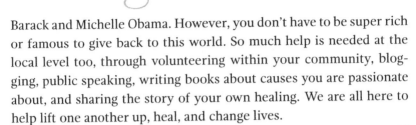

Barack and Michelle Obama. However, you don't have to be super rich or famous to give back to this world. So much help is needed at the local level too, through volunteering within your community, blogging, public speaking, writing books about causes you are passionate about, and sharing the story of your own healing. We are all here to help lift one another up, heal, and change lives.

As people wake up through self-healing, more consciousness will be created, which will increase evolved unions with a primary goal to succeed so they can help others. Right now, the world still needs so much healing. Whole partnerships are uncommon, because men and women are still being conditioned to want different things. But as the world is still changing and evolving, this too will change. What I've witnessed with my own male friends, depending on how they were raised and their family values, is that as they matured and got older, they wanted the same things as women—to love and connect. It's impossible to achieve that level of love and connection when you are only in it for yourself, running from partner to partner.

You don't give yourself time to really know anyone or allow anyone in (I go into further detail about male gender roles and how it has affected them and our relationships in the second book of the Resilient Love series). However, society conditions men to believe in the short term and that love and connection are not what they really want, and those without good role models believe it to be true. Because of this, they spend much of their lives feeling empty, restless, and depressed, trying to find what is missing. They don't realize it is love and connection they are longing for, until they find and lose real love. It is then that life shows them what they were seeking. Still, they need to face themselves first and do the inner work just as we do, to heal and know they are worthy of real love *before* they are ready for love to stay.

True healing comes when we connect to the light within us and shine that light onto our wounds. Connecting to Spirit and feeling its abundance of healing love. If you are in search of love, you are in search of the love and wholeness within that only your light, self-love and self-worth can provide. Some even say, "Well, I've had a loving relationship, but I still felt empty inside." That is because love begins within us and that is the basis of this book. The love we have been longing and searching for is the light and love that already exists within us. Real love is extending that love and sharing that light outward.

We were born for love and connection, but we cannot truly connect with another person when that connection is based on what you need from that other person. True connection takes putting our armor down. It's showing the person who you really are from your heart. It's allowing them to be who they are. It takes trust and respect. You cannot have connection without openness, trust, and respect, and that takes vulnerability and bravery. And it is there you find the magic and beauty of connection.

When we are connected with our light within us, we are able to better connect with our partners. The eternal light that shines within all of us. Just mention this and something lights up within you. The love you have always been seeking already exists inside you. All roads lead to us seeking that light (love) whether you choose to do it positively or negatively. Down the positive roads you will find spiritual connection and work. Down the negative roads of drugs, alcohol, sex, and other numbing activities, you will remain in search of what is missing. The choice is always yours.

For us to heal as a society, we need to stop playing our toxic, unhealed gender roles that have been plaguing us for centuries. Women are not the only ones who have been victimized. Men would not wound women, or other men unless they too, were wounded. It is their unhealed wounds and unhealthy patterns that have ruled society, but we are now slowly healing more than ever before.

When I first started writing this book, there wasn't a lot of material about men rising up. Now, we are seeing a surge of brave men rising-up, recognizing the damaging effects of the negative side of masculine behavior that surrounded them growing up. Beliefs that are hurtful to themselves, and to women. Men are now rising up and are boldly saying, "Hey man, I feel. And it's okay to feel. It's okay to express when I've been hurt. I don't have to 'man up.' It's okay to love and want love and not just want sex. It's okay to be human man." On social media, I think of Mark Groves at *Create the Love*, *The Better Man Project*, the documentary, *The Mask You Live in*; motivational speakers such as Price Ea, and Jay Shetty. I also want to give shout outs to Ken Nwadike Jr of the *Free Hugs Project*, actor Justin Baldoni, and spiritual

poet, Yung Pueblo. Yung Pueblo does beautiful work in expressing the light, pain, and healing of this journey in his book *Inward*.

Bad boys are out, emotionally healthy, conscious men, are the new sexy. These men are rising up to support women too, acknowledging where men have behaved poorly with women as well.

For years, men who think of themselves as "players," have preyed on women by connecting with them emotionally. Pretending to be vulnerable, and "getting it," knowing that this tactic works to get women to fall for them. What these players don't realize is how much they are shorting changing themselves. Real conscious, emotionally healthy, men know love and playing with someone's heart is not a game. Love is real and such a beautiful amazing gift, and because they have this understanding, they get so much real love and real respect in return. So, in the end, the player only played himself, because he has no real love or real respect in life.

Many men are awakening to the fact that it takes a lot more courage to express what they feel, what they love, than to be suppressed by a society that still does not fully accept it, and would rather men suppress it and hide behind anger and shame. Then we wonder why male suicide is one of the leading causes of death (I shed more light onto the toxic side of masculinity and male suicide in my next book Resilient Love: Moving Forward).

Women are rising up and finding their voice through the resurgence of the feminist movement in full vigor for equal rights, Times Up, #metoo, Wonder Woman, and Fearless Girl—the bronze statue of a young girl who stood boldly, staring down at the raging bronze bull sculpture in the heart of the heavily male-dominated culture of Wall Street. She was later relocated nearby to the New York Stock Exchange, after taking a tour through Europe. She is an icon for young women and the future of women.

What we are witnessing are the masculine and feminine energies waking up and rising within us, if we are feeling the call. However, we won't be able to heal women, or society, unless we help our brothers heal too. We all need healing, and as more of us heal, this healing will reflect on society.

Men and women can both carry heathy and unhealthy masculine and feminine energy.

Healthy Masculine Energy	Unhealthy Masculine Energy
Action, focus, drive, vision, strength, healthy risk taking, discipline, responsible, determined, assertive, goal oriented, leader, supportive, stable	Anger, bullying, controlling, proud, foolish, unhealthy risk taking, predator, cowardice, victim mentality, needy, inattentive, unreasonable, narrow minded.

Healthy Feminine Energy	Unhealthy Feminine Energy
Intuitive, feeling, expressive, communicative, nurturing, kind, caring, understanding, selfless, flexible, organized, collaborative, creative, flow, ease, allowing, patient.	Smothering, powerless, manipulative, co-dependency, uncaring, doormat, gossipy, blame, withholding, passive.

Soul Energy/True Self
Love, peace, wisdom, compassion, unity, expansion, purpose.

When energy is unbalanced in us and in the world, as it is now, the unhealthy energy will feel aggressive. Once the male and female energies balance out within us and in our society, it will bring forth more cohesion into the world.

Heart-based People vs. Fear-based People

When I was going through my divorce, I joined a divorce support group. There were many guys there who became good friends. We were like a big family. It made me realize that men had feelings, just like women, and they experienced hurt in relationships, just like women. Each of these men moved on to have wonderful relationships, and even children. I couldn't be happier for them. This is what made me realize that men and women weren't so far apart. We are all human beings. Some are more mature, whole, and heart-centered people who can form healthy relationships, while others are more wounded, immature, ego and fear-based, who can't develop healthy relationships. This applies to all genders.

Heart-based people need to find other heart-based people to make it work. In theory, if everyone placed higher standards on the people they date, it would force unhealthy people to seek help sooner, because they wouldn't have anyone to date! But the opposite is true right now. So many people not only tolerate toxic behavior in a relationship, they fight for that person to love them back.

Dating After Divorce

I am actually enjoying dating after divorce and at an older age, because I've learned so much and I think others who have divorced have learned too. It removes most of the superficiality and immaturity we had in our twenties. It has been a humbling experience for all of us. Most of the men out there dating in their 40s and 50s have ex-wives and children from that marriage. Depending on the man's emotional age, most older, divorced men (not all) want to find a partner again, rather than get out there and play the field. As they've gotten older, many realized how important it is to form that connection and they try to pass down what they've learned to their kids. Life is the greatest teacher.

~ ~ ~

Self-Love/Self-Care Exercises

Affirmation: *"I love and accept myself as I am. Today, I will start treating myself as I would my own best friend."*

Self-love music: "This Girl is on Fire," by Alicia Keys

Self-love pocket reminder: Your pocket reminder can be the word "Compassion" or the affirmation, "I accept myself as I am. I am whole and complete within myself."

Altar prep:
This week you will set up your altar with words and symbols of what self-love means to you. This can be images of self-love, things you love that bring you joy. Photos, words, rose quartz crystals, mala beads, flowers, etc.

Day 1—Self-Love

Affirmation: *"I love and honor myself so much that I choose to release what is no longer serving my highest good."*

Self-care action: Choose at least one self-care action step from the list in Lesson 4.

Self-love exercise: Journal. Answer as many questions as you wish from the list of Self-Love questions below.

I know this may seem like a lot, so take your time. Go at your own pace. You can always come back later. Your answers can be as long or as short as you want. Usually one or two sentences will be fine, unless a lot of things are coming up for you and you want to get them out.

Writing is always more beneficial, but if you don't want to write, contemplate on the questions that resonate with you most throughout the day. Don't skip this important exercise.

Self-love questions:

- In what ways have I not been loving to myself or being my own best friend?
- How does this serve me?
- Do I want to be happy? Y/N
- Am I willing to do what it takes to be happy? Even if it means loving myself? Y/N
- What steps will get me there?
- How would treating myself as my own best friend benefit me?
- In what ways have I not been accepting myself?
- How would accepting myself and not being so hard on myself make my life happier and easier on me?
- Where did the negative thoughts about myself originate? Whose voice is it that is judging me and being unkind? How will knowing where they come from allow me to distance myself from this voice and realize it is not mine? Was it magazines, friends, a parent?

- In what ways have I made other people's perceived opinions of me more important than my own?
- How will defining who I am help me to be happier and free?
- In what ways have I been judging myself?
- In what ways have I been projecting judgments about myself onto others? How can I recognize when I do that in the future?
- How does trying to understand and face a trigger, rather than quickly running away, help me become more resilient to it and help me to grow? What tools can I use?
- How does knowing the balance between facing a trigger to heal vs. knowing when to walk away serve my highest good? What limit can I set for myself?
- Why am I attracted to people who are not good for me, hurt me, or show that they do not really care about or love me?
- Why have I stayed in relationships that were unhealthy for me?
- What do my past relationships tell me about myself? What patterns are there?
- Do I fall for wounded people? What can I learned from my past relationships?
- How does knowing when to walk away from a situation or relationship serve me well, serve my highest good?
- How is making better choices in partners for myself an act of self-love?
- In what ways will I honor myself moving forward?
- How is awareness my superpower?
- From a scale of 1 to 10, how much do I love myself? What can I do to raise the bar a little each day?
- How proud am I of myself for how far I've come?

Altar

Meditation ▪ Prayer ▪ Intentions

Go to your altar and set up the words or inspiration for this week, what it means to love yourself. Light the candle. Say a prayer or meditate on feeling good and loving yourself for how far you've come in your journey and to your highest good.

Mala beads

If you have mala beads, you can use them for this meditation practice. If you don't have mala beads, you can buy them at an affordable price online. Etsy is a good place to start. There are 108 beads, plus a guru bead in the center. During meditation touch each bead and recite a mantra. You can use, "I love myself" or "I am love." Repeat this 108 times. Do not cross the guru bead. Turn the mala around and start over again. Wear your favorite essential oil that reminds you of love as you meditate. Lavender and rose oil are good oils for love.

Day 2

Affirmation: *"I know my self-worth. I am deserving of the infinite love and abundance the Universe has to offer me."*

Self-care action: Choose at least one self-care action step from the list in Lesson 4.

Self-love exercise: Journal. Answer as many questions as you wish from the list of Self-Love questions below.

Self-love questions:

- Are you aware of all that you deserve?
- How is wanting what you deserve different from knowing what you deserve?
- How is knowing you are worthy of love and all the things this world has to offer an act of self-love?
- What does having what you deserve look like? Dream big! Be bold and daring about what you want. What does it feel like?
- What can you start doing today to get there now?
- How will staying committed to yourself and this path get you there?

When we know and truly believe in what we deserve, we send a message out to the Universe that will match that energy.

Altar

Meditation ▪ Prayer ▪ Intentions

Light the candle. Say a prayer or meditate on how you are deserving of all that you have been inspired to desire and what it would feel like to have it.

Day 3

Affirmation: *"I love myself, so I choose what's best for my growth every day."*

Self-care action: Choose at least one self-care action step from the list in Lesson 4.

Self-love exercise: Journal. Answer as many questions as you wish from the list of Self-Love questions below.

Self-love Questions
Self-love internal check:

- How have I been showing up for myself?
- Am I honoring myself, accepting myself and forgiving myself?
- Have I been treating myself as I would my own best friend?
- List all the things you love about yourself. Yes, do it! There are plenty of things to love about yourself.
- Are you compassionate?
- Do you like to help others?
- Are you a good friend?
- Do you love you for the work that you are doing here and showing up for yourself?
- Do you love that you are learning to set loving boundaries for yourself?
- Do you love that you are no longer allowing other people or the media to define you?
- Do you love that you can now walk away from what is not serving your highest good?
- What do you honestly love about yourself that you've never allowed yourself to say before because you thought it was too self-centered? Start owning it.

Writing the answers to these questions may seem uncomfortable or silly at first, which is even more of a reason to get comfortable with what you love about yourself, and let it sink in.

Altar

Meditation ▪ Prayer ▪ Intentions

Light the candle. Say a prayer or meditate, setting the intention on how much you love yourself and are dedicated to your self-growth and this path. Add the words of self-love that you wrote to your altar. Take in your own loving presence. You can play your favorite music that gets you in this mood. Mediate for 10 to 20 minutes.

You can listen to the free bonus self-love meditation I created for you on the Resilient Love website at:

karenOM.com/resilient-love-meditations
Password: resilientlover

Day 4

Affirmation: "I love my life. I love myself. I choose to be wholeheart-edly single until the right partner comes into my life."

Self-care Action: Choose at least one self-care action step from the list in Lesson 4.

Self-love exercise: Journal. Answer as many questions as you wish from the list of Self-Love questions below.

Self-love questions:

- In what ways are you honoring yourself by staying single until you meet the right person, rather than settling for less than what you want?
- How does self-love help you raise your standards?
- How can self-love help you recognize partners who aren't right for you?
- How does self-love help you recognize partners who are right for you?
- How does self-love show a potential partner you value and respect yourself?
- How does self-love raise your worth?
- How will being authentically *you* attract the right partners to you, rather than you trying to be who you think someone else wants to get them to like you?
- In what ways are you honoring yourself by only dating people deserving of your love?
- How is someone's need of you not really about loving you but about them?
- In what ways are you honoring yourself by only dating people whom you would like to pursue a relationship with? Not being with someone simply to fill a void.
- How does dating someone only to be with someone keeping you from the love you do want?

- How is dating someone who is crazy about you, but you're just passing time until someone better comes along, perpetuate the cycle of hurt?
- How would it feel to genuinely love someone for who they are, rather than your need for them?
- How does it make you feel when you are honoring yourself in dating and relationships vs. when you are not?
- How does loving, honoring, and supporting yourself without the need of someone else to make you feel happy, whole, and complete set you free?

Altar

Meditation ▪ Prayer ▪ Intentions

Light the candle. Say a prayer or meditate on how you are honoring yourself by choosing to live a wholeheartedly single life until you meet the right partner.

Day 5

Affirmation: *"I choose to live my life, not in the way anyone else thinks I should live my life, but in the way my truest highest self chooses to live it."*

Self-care action: Choose at least one self-care action step from the list in Lesson 4.

Self-love exercise: Journal. Answer as many questions as you wish from the list of Self-Love questions below.

Self-love questions:

- In what ways has practicing self-love benefitted you?
- In what ways can you love yourself more?
- How will being more authentic free you from what was holding you back and empower your best self?
- In what ways are you being more authentic?
- Are you speaking your truth? Remember, speaking your truth isn't being "all up in someone's face," but honoring your thoughts, opinions, and feelings to be as valid and as important as anyone else's. It's being the boss of you and not allowing others to be in charge.
- In what ways do you still feel unsafe being you and need to step into your power? What steps (baby steps) can you challenge yourself to get there?
- How does finding the balance between being authentically you from your truest highest self (a place of love) and not from spiritual ego (a place of fear, puffing up) keep you more grounded, heart-centered, and authentic.

Altar

Meditation ▪ Prayer ▪ Intentions

Light the candle. Say a prayer or meditate on how you are honoring yourself for being authentically you.

Day 6

Affirmation: *"I choose to live from my highest self every day."*

Self-care action: Choose at least one self-care action step from the list in Lesson 4.

Self-love exercise: Journal. Answer as many questions as you wish from the list of Self-Love questions below.

Self-love questions:

- What differences am I noticing within myself from this week that I am really enjoying?
- How has taking care of myself first benefited my life and my relationships?
- How can I live more from my highest self and make sure my soul is honored every day?
- How can I be more creative with my self-love and self-care? Creativity breeds inspiration. Creativity comes from the soul, and it doesn't just mean painting, music, or dance. It's also writing and doing something uniquely you that comes from your heart.

Altar

Meditation • Prayer • Intentions

Light the candle. Say a prayer or meditate on how you are honoring yourself by choosing to live to your highest good and for the highest good for all. Today, you may use your meditation bonus gift I created for you on my website at:

karenOM.com/resilient-love-meditations
Password: resilientlover

Day 7

You can use this day to catch up on an exercise, or use it as day to reflect on what you learned before advancing to the next.

Continue the habit of developing and staying with your own practice.

Bonus:

One of my favorite and easy self-love meditations you can do anytime is breathing in love and feeling that energy fill your body. If you are going through a difficult time, breathe love into the part of you that needs that love, breathe out all the love you feel inside and release that energy, sending all that love out into the world. This will help you to become ready for our next Lesson on Love is Everywhere.

Love Is Everywhere

*Look at the world with bright eyes and you
will begin to notice that the love you have
been seeking was already all around you*

Love Is Everywhere!

This week may not be as intense as the others; it might even be fun. However, this week serves a purpose just as great, if not greater, than the others. Without this step, the work would be incomplete. We've released what no longer serves us making space for something new and good to come in. You have ignited your inner light. You've done the work. You've done so much of the heavy lifting, now you're ready to allow the good stuff to come through, and you deserve it!

We covered the common myth that you need a partner in order to be complete and be happy. You now know that couldn't be further from the truth. You know you are already whole and complete as you are, even without a partner. We also know that needing love from a partner in order to fulfill you, more often than not, leads to the type of love you don't want. We know relationships are two whole people who complement each other, loving the other person for who they are, rather than who we need them to be; these are examples of authentic love. Love blossoms from who you both already are. When the foundation of love is built on a need for it, it won't be long before you or your partner focus on

what you're not doing for them. When both partners are complete, the focus is on each other's strengths and supporting one another.

If you get anything out of this book, my wish is that you walk away with the following:

- Know you are not incomplete without a partner; you are already whole and complete as you are.
- You are worthy and deserving of all that you want.
- To always honor and respect yourself.
- To accept who and where you are, while striving for more.
- Know the answers are all within you. You have the power.
- Be aware of your assignments and lessons. Everyone is your teacher.
- You are not your past but the light that shines in you.
- You are never alone. God, the Universe has an infinite amount of love and guidance for you, you only need to stay connected to it.

We went from knowing that love wasn't only in our romantic relationships but that it exists within us too. This week, we are going to increase our awareness even further to seeing that love is already all around us too! It's everywhere!

Americans seem to put all the focus on romantic love. The English language only has one word for love that is supposed to encompass all types of love, whereas the Greeks have eight words for all different kinds of love.

Eros: Passion, possession, lust.
Ludus: Love is a game. No commitment.
Pragma: Enduring love, as in marriage.
Philia: Love between friends.
Storge: Family love.
Philautia: Self-love both positive and negative.
Meraki: Putting your soul into your work. Do something with love.
Agape: Unconditional love and spiritual (God) love.

Maybe if the English language had as many definitions of love, we Americans wouldn't be so confused about the type of relationships we are in, and whether we are aligned with the type of love we want. We would have a better idea if we were in a *ludas* type of relationship and not the *pragma* love we want. We would also know that just because we didn't have pragma love, we still had *philia, storge, phlautia,* and *agape* love. We would know we are never without love.

My perception really started to shift about love when I began to understand that love wasn't just romantic, and it was already around me, all the time. I just needed to tap into it. Society conditions us to believe that the only love worth having is found in romantic relationships. Up until this point on my spiritual path, even though I was transforming my unforgiveness, victimization, and limiting beliefs from my fear-based self to my love-based self, there was still something about romantic love that I felt was missing from my life. I loved my newly found soul family, but I was still feeling a little empty inside without a partner.

What leads so many of us onto a spiritual path is often the excruciating pain that comes from heartbreak. When we are down on our knees looking for solace, the spiritual path is often the cushion, luring us in through the salvation in manifesting a soulmate. We see articles titled: "Law of attraction. Manifest your soulmate in sixty days!" and we'll try anything to find a partner to stop the painful longing for love. But for the lucky ones we find so much more. We find our inner light and divine love. We find our path.

~ ~ ~

Dating Detox and Living a Wholeheartedly Single Life

It was a cold January day in New York City. I was attending Gabby Bernstein's six-week, "May Cause Miracles" workshop at a yoga studio in Greenwich Village. Back in the day, she was still able to do small intimate workshops in yoga studios around the city. Now, Gabby needs an auditorium for 1,000 people, and even more attend via Live Stream around the world. Even though I miss the days we were in tiny cozy yoga studios, I couldn't be happier for her spreading her message with the masses. I signed up for the workshop, because I wanted to get rid of all the pain inside from my divorce. I wanted to manifest my new soulmate, even though I knew I was trying to fill my voids. I didn't care. I just wanted the hurt to go away and to be happy again. It wasn't as bad as before, now that I knew what I was doing and why I was doing it, but yet it was still there, nevertheless.

On the first day of the workshop, I remember when Gabby said, "A miracle is a shift in perception." I was thinking, "What? I don't want a shift in perception? That's not what I signed up for. This workshop is about manifesting miracles, and I want miracles! I want to manifest a new soulmate!" Oh my gosh, this is cracks me up now. Could you imagine if I demanded my money back? Gabby probably would have returned it to me, along with knowing I wasn't ready to receive the message or do the work. Thank you God that I didn't ask for my money back and I hung in there.

Now, I know a shift in perception is E-V-E-R-Y-T-H-I-N-G. The shifts I received were better than manifesting any soulmate. It was exactly what I needed, not the soulmate, because I received the lesson that helped me to be the person I needed to be to attract and create the beautiful relationship I wanted. Bam! I was eager to learn more. Now, all I want are shifts, because I gain more insight, awareness, understanding, and freedom with each shift. If you stay the course, you will continue to have more and more amazing shifts and growth too for the rest of your life.

The following day, at the end of our six weeks together, I was walking along the bay in my favorite park, feeling like I had graduated in my personal and spiritual development. Gabby had also planted a seed. Planting seeds is when an idea or a thought stays with you after the coaching session or workshop is over. The work is always done after you close the book, and after the workshop is over. It's about how you apply it in your daily life. When a seed is planted, you may not realize it at the time, but later you have an "aha" moment that can be life changing. That's what happened to me after the workshop. I continued to have miraculous shifts in perception, and I still do today.

Gabby had said during the workshop, that love was not just in your romantic relationships that love was everywhere! It was in the sky and the trees. On that walk, I looked up at the sky, and at the trees, and started placing my focus that love was in the sky, and in the trees, and I began seeing that love was everywhere! I definitely found it in my spiritual practice. And I started seeing it in the people I met every day. I knew I loved my family and friends, but I didn't consider it "real love," because it was so ingrained in me that real love was only found in a romantic partner.

We take so much of the love we have for granted. Family love, such as the love between a child and a parent or siblings is the kind of love we think is always there, that is until we lose them. The loss could be through a move or through the unimaginable. Only then do we realize how much love was there and lost, because we didn't spend time relishing it while it was still there. I didn't come to this realization until I got married and moved away from New York. I felt that I lost everything I knew and loved. Gone were my friends and family. I was so homesick. Even though, I eventually came to love Wisconsin, the feeling never really went away. There was always a little aching pit inside of me that longed for my family and my home.

Growing up, I saw my family in between seeing my friends, who were also like family to me. The impact hit me even harder when I lost my dad and my oldest sister, Marjorie; two people who always cheered me on, and I thought would always be there for me because they always were. This changed me forever. Then almost losing my mother when she was attacked at a subway station. Today, I place such an importance on spending time with my family and relishing every moment, knowing how life changes all the time, and there will never be this moment, again.

Gabby also suggested we find more romance in our friendships, which was something I've never heard of, but wanted to implement. So much time with our friends can be spent talking about how much our love lives suck. Then, when we do find love, we spend so much time talking to our friends about how much our partners suck. Ego is never happy or satisfied. I wanted to practice philia (friendship love), by applying more love, beauty, and joy into my friendships. However, something kept getting in the way, which was my own nagging belief that I still needed a romantic partner to be complete! That was the moment I decided to stop messing around.

The longing was the worst, and I knew it was only going to lead me into more dead-end situations. Not to mention, I would be miserable along the way. I didn't have a horrendous relationship track record, but there was plenty of room for improvement. I was still committed to having a beautiful, healthy relationship. Anna, my other life coach aside from Gabby, had said words that were still ringing in my ear, "You have to be healthy yourself if you want a healthy partner. A healthy person can sense an unhealthy person right away." As I write this now, on the other side of all the healing work that I've done, I know these words to be true—I can now sense unhealthy people right away. I couldn't understand this when I was unhealthy and unaware and that is exactly why I wound up in relationships and situations that did not serve my highest good.

I realized I needed to detox myself from romantic love and start treating love as an addiction. As with any other addiction, I needed to rid myself of the perception that I had to have a partner in order to be complete, and that romantic love was the only type of love in this world. Once I made that decision, it began to open my eyes to the fact that most of society was brainwashed into believing they needed a partner in order to be complete, that they weren't complete and whole unless they had a partner. We are also addicted to love (and sex) to varying degrees, in order to fill those voids with love (and/or sex) in order to feel complete. We either feel incomplete without a partner, or we have such an adverse reaction that if "love" is mentioned, there is an aversion to love; we no longer want anything to do with it. We become like an addict who rid himself of that nasty habit years ago.

Love and sexual addictions are not to be taken lightly. They can be as serious as any other addiction. Love Addicts Anonymous groups operate like any other addiction group. Love or sex is some people's drug of choice. We can be so consumed by love, but not realize how dependent we are on it, like an addiction.

Ad·dic·tion

Noun: The state of being enslaved to a habit or practice or to something that is psychologically or physically habit-forming, such as narcotics, to such an extent that its cessation causes severe trauma.

Sounds a lot like dysfunctional or wounded love.

Symptoms of a Love Addict:

- Craves and searches for love (or sex) constantly.
- Searches for a relationship when not in a relationship.
- Feels desperate and alone when not in a relationship or having enough sex.
- Finds it unbearable or emotionally difficult to be alone.
- Compulsively uses sex and fantasy to fill the loneliness when not in a relationship.
- Uses sex, seduction, and manipulation (guilt/shame) to "hook" or hold onto a partner.
- Uses sex or romantic intensity to tolerate difficult experiences or emotions (numbing).
- Misses out on important family, career, or social experiences to search for a romantic or sexual relationship.
- Uses anonymous sex, porn, or compulsive masturbation to avoid "needing" someone, thereby avoiding all relationships.

Love addicts are people who crave the feeling of love and bounce from relationship to relationship, but behind that need is a fear of intimacy. They long for love, but at the same time, they are terrified of getting too close or too vulnerable, getting hurt and allowing someone in. So, although they are desperate for love, connection, and intimacy,

they also keep it at arm's length to keep themselves safe. They may or may not even be aware they are doing it.

Again, that's how slick ego is. Just like the alcoholic, a love addict must sometimes hit rock bottom to see that their intense need for love is causing unhealthy behavior patterns in their life. It's no coincidence that love addiction meetings are combined with sex addiction meetings. Sex addicts are also seeking love and have a fear intimacy and getting too close, although they are not quite aware of it. They also use sex to fulfill the need for love and fill the void, but I get into more of that in the lesson on spirituality and sex in my next book.

These two groups are at the highest degree of love addicts. You may be at the lower end of the spectrum, but if you feel you need to have a partner, then to some degree, you are addicted to love. The majority of us are to some extent or another are but not any fault of our own we were conditioned to believe we were not good enough or whole without a partner. But it's up to us to break that cycle.

Looking at the symptoms, I met the first two criteria—"Searches for a romantic relationship when not in a relationship" and "Feels alone when not in a relationship." As they say in Alcoholics Anonymous, the first step in recovery is recognizing you have a problem. As I've said, this is what we've been taught, that we need to be in a relationship to be happy, and we were never taught otherwise, until now. What's most important is acknowledging, accepting, and healing yourself from the dependency of needing a date or a partner, so that it no longer controls your life.

I decided to put myself on a dating detox for three months. During the detox, I didn't search for or think about a new partner. I also did not look for validation from the opposite sex to make myself feel worthy. I was going to find my beauty, value, and worth within myself. My focus was only on my own healing, looking for what inspired me, seeing the beauty in each day, and enjoying my life, my family, my friends, and the world around me.

Wait! But what about sex? Believe it or not, you don't need sex to survive. You may be horny (seeking validation, connection, worthiness, filling wounds, numbing), but you are not going to die without sex. You don't need sex like you need air, water, and food to survive. The human race may die off if we all stopped having sex, but *you* specifically will not die if you don't have sex for a few months. Trust me, you will live and be better for it.

Sex is a gift. Not an activity just for pleasure. It's pleasurable, but it's purpose is not solely for pleasure. It is a beautiful exchange of loving energy between two partners that cannot be found in a hookup or casual dating. It is the most intimate expression of love we can share with someone. If we do not keep sex or our energy sacred, the most sacred things about us, then nothing is sacred. Your energy is sacred, and trust me, it is not something you want to share with merely anyone, no matter how hot you think they are. If they have dark funky energy, you can pick that up from them, along with STDs.

There are many people who "hook up" and have casual sex, who wear masks to hide their wounds. Some people don't even hide their wounds, because people fall for tortured souls who need saving. If you're an empath who picks up negative energy easily, imagine what kind of energy you are picking up from these wounded souls. If you are someone who is conscientious about protecting your energy, then this is one of the most important areas where you should be protecting your energy.

This isn't "holier than thou" talk or judgement. For true healing to occur, you need not answer to me, but to your soul. You need to be honest with yourself about whether sex has been an enlightening or a soul-sucking experience for you, or a combination of both. Does it start off feeling liberated, passionate, like there's a connection, but then turns into heartbreak and despair? You think that's how life is? People are all broken jerks. Doesn't this happen to everyone? It does happen more often to people who follow the same philosophy about hooking up and jumping into situations too fast and disregard red flags, but no, it's not how life is, and it doesn't happen to everyone.

When sex is used as a tool to fill voids for loneliness or fun or to feel love, connection, and validation, we don't make the best decisions. We become addicted to the feeling that can throw us off course of what we really want. You are in the fast-food lane of love. Hookup culture and even some spiritual circles glamorize it as sexual

liberation and freedom. It may have its purpose in healing for some people, but it's all fun and games until someone gets hurt.

Stuffing your emotions to hide the pain doesn't sound very liberating. And you wonder why your heart is aching, and you blame yourself for not being liberated enough or blame your ex for being an ass, so you go out and try it again, but with the same results and you're mentally and physically exhausted ready to swear off love forever. The thing is, you weren't looking for love, you were looking for sex, passion, fun, excitement, something to not feel so lonely, something to stop the pain.

When we try to heal ourselves, ego can often do a pendulum swing in healing from feeling victimized to doing the complete opposite and feeling empowered. Going from having no sex to lots of sex can feel empowering like you're free, but the truth and true healing always lie in the balance, not in the extremes. You don't need to have sex with lots of partners to be sexually liberated. You can have sex with one person and feel more spiritually connected and liberated than having sex with multiple partners.

What does freedom look like to you? Feel like to you?

Sex isn't wrong, but you want it to be healthy. When sex is healthy, the energy feels good and balanced. Even when the partnership ends, there is no drama; it remains beautiful and loving. It may seem less exciting, but it is more consistent. When sex is unhealthy, it's full of highs and lows and inconsistency. Your energy is depleted; there is often a lot of drama and trauma. Leaving an emptiness, a craving, and a need to find someone else to fill the void and thus repeating the cycle. A feeling similar to needing a fix. Sometimes you wind up with the same wrong partner again, or a new one, or a series of new ones to distract you from what you don't want to feel. The distraction makes you feel like you are in control and handling it, but you are not handling it. You're avoiding it. Your heart is so closed you wouldn't give your heart to anyone because you don't trust anyone with it, it's still too raw and wounded.

You're beginning to understand more than ever now through your growth, as you listen to your soul, that it wasn't the best way for you. Wisdom is telling you now, you were not ready emotionally, mentally, or physically to be with anyone until you heal your heart.

What you really need is to take time out to nurture it and give it the proper attention it's been asking for to heal which is what led many of you here.

Sex (dating and relationships) is unhealthy when it is used to avoid what we don't want to feel, or you need it to validate your worth. It gives you a false sense of security and empowerment, but it's slowly eating away at your soul, and with each experience, you feel more and more guarded; you feel like giving up. You are either on or off and it's exhausting you.

Healing comes from facing your wounds head-on and connecting with the parts of you that are telling you, you're "not good enough," "you're not worthy of real love," "you can't trust anyone with your heart, or that "no one could love the real you."

You have been playing that tape in your head for so long you've brainwashed yourself into believing those false stories to be true, and then ego found everything it could to confirm it to be true. But it's not true. You are worthy of real love. And someone would absolutely love the real you. However, until you believe it yourself, you will give no one else a chance until you believe it too. Not only that, you will reject everyone who does love you and seek validation from those who don't. And if you find someone who does love you, you won't believe it's true and you subconsciously do what you can to sabotage the relationship out of distrust that anyone could love you to prove yourself right.

If you want to be free, finally, you have to brainwash yourself into knowing you are worthy of the love you want and deserve. You have to fight for it for yourself. And to get there, you must let go of anything that does not look like the love you want. You have to love, honor, and respect yourself first every day. Remember, you are the gatekeeper of your life. You are in control and responsible for who you allow into your life. No more blaming people who show you tons of red flags and hurt you, but you continue to go back to them. From now on, you must make a vow to yourself to allow only those who are worthy of your love into your life. Don't cheapen your worth by making those who are not worthy, worthy. Not everybody is worthy when it comes to romantic love and sex. You must commit to yourself every day in order to undo the subconscious wiring that is telling you otherwise.

True healing comes when we connect to that light within us and shine light onto our wounds. Connecting to Spirit and feeling its abundance of healing love. If you are in a search for love, you are in search of the love and wholeness within that only your light and the love of Spirit can heal. When you are searching for love and connection through a stream of unhealthy relationships and sex, what you are really looking for is connection; to feel that love and wholeness, that is within yourself, but you keep trying to find it through someone else, rather than through your own light. Then everything else will fall into place.

When you try to find love in unhealthy ways, you will always end up feeling exhausted and yearning for love. When you search for love through your light and connection with Spirit, you will always feel fulfilled and free. Have you ever felt that tremendous awe-inspiring feeling that only comes when you connect with God and the Universe? The Japanese have a word for it, *Yugen*, "the awareness of the Universe that triggers a response too powerful and deep for words." It's that feeling when something is so beautiful it brings tears to your eyes. Sometimes lots of tears. It is in that moment you feel the immense non-judgmental unconditional love this energy has for all of us. All of us. Whatever your beliefs or experiences have been in the past with God, Spirit or the Universe, allow this loving energy to flow through you the best way you can receive it. This force of loving energy does not seek to judge or punish you, but wants you to find your way home to help you heal and to love you. Whatever you have been told otherwise, is untrue. You were created exactly as you were meant to be. When you connect to this loving energy, there is no feeling of lack. When I am connected to this energy, I feel an immediate sense of forgiveness for all my false and foolish egoic beliefs and so much love. I feel lighter, whole, abundant, and free.

People on a spiritual path would agree that the Dalai Lama is among one of the most spiritual people in the world and he has taken a vow of chastity. Buddhist monks all practice celibacy. No, I am not saying you have to become celibate, but rather to make a point that they know sex is not the answer to fulfillment, but can be the cause of suffering and attachment. Buddhist have let go of all the external things man thinks is fulfillment in order to find true fulfillment and peace within. And instead have picked up love, kindness, and compassion. When we let go of all of the limiting beliefs that are ingrained in us, that our value only comes from having a partner, what we look like or what we have, that is when we make space for true freedom and more peace, love, happiness, and fulfillment in our lives.

When we are whole and lit from within, sex is something beautiful to share and express. It gives, it doesn't need. The connection nourishes your soul; it doesn't deplete it.

Only you can determine if sex is something you use to feel validated and fill voids, but pay close attention, because ego can be really slick in getting its needs met and convincing you otherwise. Needing a fix and feeling the crash afterward, like any addiction, is a good indication. Trust that your highest self will know whether it is working for you or against you. That is part of your personal growth and healing journey.

I get more into the spiritual aspect of sex in the second book of the Resilient love series, but right now, let's discuss it as part of our detox from dating and relationships, while recognizing how dependent we are on it to validate us and fill our voids.

What I discovered at the end of my six-month detox was amazing. Yes, six months! I had reached the end of my three-month mark and added another three months. I don't even count how long it's been between dates anymore. It's insignificant to me. I don't judge myself for going on a date or not going on a date. Because of the dating detox, I was able to be fully present when I was with my friends and family. My mind wasn't wandering, feeling partially incomplete, like I was killing time until I met "the one." I was able to really enjoy life rather than feeling like I was just occupying my time until life really began. Are you familiar with that feeling? After you finally get married and divorced, you realize what a crock that is. However, I could still identify that same longing in some of my single friends who wanted to meet a partner, while they killed time with me. This is the friend who drops you the minute they get a date. That's where they are. They have to be ready to see it. That is their journey.

When one client I had finally broke her addiction, it was so amazing to see her transformation, as she went from someone who was unhappy, frustrated, and desperately dating one person after another, having unfulfilling casual sex, to someone who was smiling, joyfully single, and enjoying her life fully present, until the right partner comes along. That, my friend, is the miracle and gift of the shift in perception. Nothing changed, other than her beliefs around love. She had the same life, same house, same job, and still no boyfriend; the only a difference was her perspective. And she is now so much happier, much more relaxed, and enjoying life.

You can go through life in survival mode, being wholly consumed by it, or you can choose to fully enjoy life now, as it is. I remember when I was in college, sitting around the dinner table with my family. I couldn't wait until it was over so I could get up and leave to hang out with my friends. What I wouldn't do today to have an evening with my dad and sister. I treasure every moment I have with my family now.

After the dating detox, I no longer felt that deep ache that something or someone was missing in my life. My independence came easily and naturally. The yearning and emptiness were gone. I didn't have to be with someone to feel complete. I only go out with people whose values and hopes and dreams align with mine, where I believe we would be a complement to each other's lives. Yes, I have passed up a lot of cute and successful guys along the way, who the old me would have totally dated only to realize what a huge mistake it was. Superficial interactions are out, only true soulful connections for this girl. I don't have to make a mistake ten times anymore to figure out what's not working. I know who is right for me and who is not. Dating is not a numbers game when you know what you want, instead you become aligned with it.

I don't feel self-conscious walking into parties or public places without a partner. I don't mind being the third, fifth, or even the seventh wheel with friends. I am not defined by whether I am with a partner or not. It's rare for anyone to even ask me if I'm dating or why I'm not. I think I put out the vibe that I am happy with my life, and I'm only available for the right one. If someone does ask me the question, I know it's just a projection of their own beliefs that they need a partner to be complete, rather than me not being complete as an individual.

Going on a dating detox and living a wholeheartedly single life allows me to choose someone I really like, rather than someone I need. It has also given me a better sense and ability to walk away from relationships that do not serve my highest good.

As I mentioned in the Dating Detox introduction, the detox is an important step in this process for so many reasons, even if you haven't been dating because you stopped dating because you are heartbroken by your ex, or because you are tired of men and the dating scene and taking a break, or sworn off men; technically, even though you aren't dating, you had a very specific reason for why you weren't dating. You did not kill the addiction or shift your mindset to one that says you don't need a partner to make you complete, because it wasn't in your awareness to do so.

The difference with the dating detox is, now that you've been on it, your awareness shifts to how whole and complete you are without a partner. The purpose is to enjoy your life, knowing that love is all around you, not just in your romantic relationships, but in your friendships and with your family. It's in nature and in the things you love to do. It's knowing you are more than enough.

You are already whole and complete as you are.

~ ~ ~

Wholeness Can Be Found in Your Purpose

(If you are not feeling connected to a life purpose, or you may already know what your purpose is, you may skip this lesson and move on to "Your Path and Your Partner.")

"Every woman who heals herself helps to heal all the women
who came before her and all those who come after."
~ Dr. Christiane Northrup

While I was on my dating detox, I increased my self-love practice by recognizing all the love that was already all around me all the time and staying connected to the magnificent power and beauty of the Universe. Knowing in that moment when we are connected, we feel all of the magic and love of the Universe; we lack for nothing. I believe this is what heaven must feel like when we transition back home.

It is in this space when I remain open that I receive so many messages. This was when it was revealed to me that I had a purpose of bringing how I healed to others—so that others could heal their hearts and become resilient in love. I discovered during this awakening, this journey and detox, that the part I had been missing was within me all along. Instead of looking outward for love and validation through others to make me feel whole and worthy, I found it through my healing, my connection to my higher-self, and my divine purpose. Our work here on Earth is to learn how to heal our wounds and teach others to do the same, so we do not continue passing down wounds to other generations; instead, we pass down light and healing. When we are still unaware or wounded, we spend so much time searching to fill that missing piece we feel inside, through romantic relationships or in material wealth and competing with each other for it, effecting our self-worth and being reactive to it. Because that is what this current society taught us. There's nothing wrong with wanting those things, but they are bonuses. It's in the awareness of understanding that those things won't make you happy or feel fulfilled until you are already happy and fulfilled within yourself. It is in healing and waking up that we realize that what we were missing is not in getting but in giving.

As Jim Carrey says, "I wish everyone could get rich and famous and everything they ever dreamed of so they can see that's not the answer."

Society ingrains in us that our happiness is found in success, how we look, what we wear, what we drive, where we live, etc. We are barraged with images of enormous wealth, success, fame, and fake beauty. And yet millions of people achieve this status and find they are still unhappy. For some, and maybe the lucky ones, life brings us to our knees, forcing us to look at ourselves, and we find when we were in it for ourselves, we never found happiness, we never felt fulfilled.

Each time I took a step, the next step would appear. When I sat down to write, all of this started flowing out of me. It felt natural, but I can't say the entire process has been easy, because I am still trying to unlearn ego habits that keep me distracted, but I hear it's part of the process! As I started to feel more confident with my ability to deliver my message to help people, I started having a hard time not sharing my message. I started receiving messages intuitively, gifts from the Universe on how I was to deliver this message, and what messages I was to share. This book, my blog, and social media posts are an excellent example of that.

Whether anyone "Liked" or commented on my posts, it was no longer about me, but about the people I serve, whether it be one or one million. This is my purpose during my time on Earth. However, your journey may be very different. But I, along with thousands of others, are here to shed more light into this world and help transform fear into faith. I imagine as I grow, change, and evolve, so will my messages.

This is why you are seeing a rise in the healing arts of mindfulness, meditation, yoga, reiki, spiritual coaching, and health and wellness. Yoga and meditation are now being offered in more schools, corporate offices, police stations, military bases, and even prisons. This is to help counteract all the darkness you see coming up in the world today. Just as in us, the darkness needs to surface so that we can clear it.

Maybe you had no idea you even had a life's purpose or knew what it was until you read this section, but you can feel something stirring in you now. You feel this resonating in your soul. You feel a little twinge that you are being called to do something. That twinge is your sign to build on it and explore it. While others have known for a long time what they've been called to do and are doing it, this book may be another part of their healing process, expanding their awareness on this journey. I also know there are people who have done tons of healing work, and they still feel like they don't know what their purpose is? They have been searching to the point of frustration. Please do not fret or be discouraged. Your frustration is not serving you or the world. Our purpose here is mainly to help one another, lift each other up, to be kinder, more compassionate, and respectful to one another—to bring more love, peace, and joy into this world. To be less judgmental and more accepting and understanding of others in our daily lives, what could be more healing than that?

Your purpose may not be a full-time job, but everyone healing and sharing their light with others is equally important, and our full-time purpose here on Earth.

You do not need to be trained or certified as a teacher to serve.

A Course in Miracles states, "A teacher of God is anyone who chooses to be one." And we need more teachers of love in this world. You can serve by being more compassionate at work, in traffic, at the grocery store, whenever you are out in public. You can volunteer for a cause that is important to you, or by holding a drive or fundraiser — doing anything that uplifts people or helps to bring a community together.

We also serve greatly by raising children who are more conscious, kinder, and more aware, for they will be carrying this work and the world forward in the future. Healing is not only in our emotional and mental wellness but in our physical wellness, too, from exercise to the foods we put into our bodies that can heal or harm us. Healing is also needed in our environment. Our planet desperately needs our help. We are killing the very world we live in with plastic and chemicals. We are being called to create change in so many areas to help heal our world. You can serve by supporting local organic farmers, small businesses, and reducing your use of plastic and plastic waste. How you spend your money also directs the trends that manufacturers follow.

If you decide you want to go the life coach or meditation teacher route. I highly recommend professional certification in your area of interest. The most incredible thing about training in any type of healing modality is as you are being trained to heal others, you are healing and elevating yourself too. But you have to show up and do the work because you can't effectively help heal other people if you haven't healed those parts of yourself first. It is important that we teach from our healing, not from our wounds. When we are triggered, we teach from our wounds. We inadvertently trigger and pass those wounds onto others. Ego loves to teach and tell others how to stand in their power through blame and protection. The energy feels victimized, angry, and constricted.

When we teach from our healing, we teach growth and expansion. It feels freeing. You have to understand the work yourself because you will only be able to take people as far as you have gone yourself. But the good news is, it doesn't mean you can't start now, and it doesn't mean you have to wait until you are completely healed. If that were true, then no one would be doing this work. No one is completely healed. It's a never-ending process. You can help to heal others who you are just one step behind you in the process, and as they see your progress, it will encourage them to do the same. The amazing thing about healing work is—as you teach, the more you learn, and the deeper the understanding you receive. That means everything you are going through is helping you understand, so you can transform and teach someone else to do the same.

> *"Use me, God. Show me how to take who I am,*
> *who I want to be, and what I can do, and use it*
> *for a purpose greater than myself."*
> ~ Rev. Martin Luther King, Jr.

As *A Course in Miracles* explains, in the spiritual realm, teaching is the opposite, the teacher is the student where you get the test first; then, you understand the lesson. The world is your classroom, and everyday life is trying to teach you something through what you are experiencing. Your teachers are not only the ones you choose but the ones you have attracted through your universal lessons. What you gain from it is your lesson that you can teach others how you overcame.

But if you want to be guided to something more specific, you can set your intention and ask the Universe to reveal it to you. You will recognize your purpose because it will light you up, inspire you, and bring you joy to share with others. But do not force it. Your purpose will always come to you as the Universe sees fit until then, let go and practice sharing love and compassion with others. Some of us feel we have been called to answer our purpose in a very specific way. No one can judge another person's purpose because we are all being called to serve in different ways. We each carry a piece of the puzzle. No one's purpose is greater or smaller, as no piece of a puzzle has more significance than another.

Connecting to a Power Greater Than You

I start my day, every day with these three prayers. Shared with me by Gabby Bernstein. Starting my day with these prayers has made such a huge difference in my life. I have not missed a day reciting these prayers since I received them.

Prayer 1

> *I am here only to be truly helpful.*
> *I am here to represent Him Who sent me.*
> *I do not have to worry about what to say or what to do,*
> *because He Who sent me will direct me.*
> *I am content to be wherever He wishes, knowing*
> *He goes there with me. I will be healed as I let*
> *Him teach me to heal.*
> *— A Course in Miracles*

Prayer 2: Prayer of St. Francis of Assisi

Lord, make me an instrument of thy peace.
Where there is hatred, let me sow love;
where there is injury, pardon;
where there is doubt, faith;
where there is despair, hope;
where there is darkness, light;
where there is sadness, joy.

O Divine Master,
grant that I may not so much seek
to be consoled as to console;
to be understood, as to understand;
to be loved, as to love.

For it is in giving that we receive;
it is in pardoning, that we are pardoned;
it is in dying that we are born to eternal life.

Prayer 3

What would you have me do?
Where would you have me go?
What would you have me say,
and to whom?
— A Course in Miracles

When we feel loved, supported, and inspired, we are connected. All-day, I put my focus and attention on staying connected to God, the Universe, and angels, while I'm walking down the street, driving in my car, getting dressed in the morning, and even while writing this book. I ask God, my angels, and the Universe, "What would you have me say? What do you want them to know?" and the words flow through my fingertips. I also connect with God and my angels before each coaching session so I may deliver the right message my clients need to hear to heal, move forward or feel inspired.

Receiving Messages

Our intuition is one of the ways God, the Universe, and angels send messages to you. When do they do it? For me, they always seem to send me downloads, which are epiphanies and ideas that guide me to carry out and fulfill my joy and purpose. I usually get downloads while I'm on my daily walk along the bay, while driving alone in my car, and when I'm in the shower washing my hair. It's usually when I am not anywhere near a pen to jot down everything. The Universe has a great sense of humor. I think it cracks them up to see me running around half-naked to grab a pen and take notes. These moments could also be when I am most open to receiving messages too.

You can begin sharing your messages on social media or simply by being you and allowing people to see the transformation of your own life. Practice sharing your light and your message without any need for likes or approvals. But be grateful for any approvals or likes is a good habit to get in, remembering it's not about you or your popularity but for the healing of the people you serve.

Trust whoever needs the message will receive it. Even if you get zero "Likes," be grateful for this gift you have. Someone is always listening and watching, even though they may never say anything to you. You are planting seeds. People who have never commented on any of my posts message me to tell me that my posts helped them in some way. Some people tell me they save my posts so they can refer to them again later, and one person told me that at the end of a hard day, she likes to relax and read my posts. For some people, you may be the only positive message they receive. That is who you are doing this for, not the naysayers. Don't let the naysayers distract you.

Being authentic and sharing your message, as Brené Brown would say, takes courage. You have to risk being vulnerable, and it is there you will find your strength. I do try to make sure the messages I put out there move people forward toward healing or positive action. Not everyone will get your message, and that's okay. But, if I see, I have unintentionally triggered some people I may take the post down. On some days, my energy may be off, and I want to be careful not to pass that energy onto someone else. If you are doing this work, always be responsible for the energy you are putting out there. As you continue to share your messages, your inspiration will grow stronger but remember not to force your message onto anyone. Some people may not be ready to receive it, no matter how much this work has changed your life. They may resent it, and it will only drain you of your energy. A message can only be received if the person is open and ready to receive your message. Our messages are as unique as we are, and they are not for everyone.

I'll be honest; there are some well-known amazing teachers my friends adore and swear by, who do not resonate with me. Just as some of my teachers may not resonate with someone else. I don't think it takes anything away from the teacher. It's just that they weren't for us, and we weren't for them. We each are assigned to different teachers who are as unique as we are. However, when someone is open to receiving your message, you can feel the energy of spirit moving through the both of you. It's such a beautiful and amazing experience.

It's no coincidence that we have all this technology to help us reach each other and reach around the world through the internet with podcasts, blogs, social media, and self-publishing. We have more power than we think. We are no longer dependent on radio and publishers who control our messages. We have the ability to spread our own messages.

And it's working as our sisters (and brothers) all over the world are responding. Women in Sudan, India, Honduras, South Korea,

Afghanistan, and in the Philippines are watching women here in the western world rise up for their rights, and it's giving them encouragement and permission to have a voice too. All because they have access to the internet. We hear a lot about the future being female, but it doesn't have to be either-or, what we need to work on is a future that includes all of us. We are all together in this world. It's time we start acting like it.

This healing of the world will not happen overnight. We are only at the beginning of this global shift in raising consciousness. It's not going to happen by just demanding laws to be changed. We all have our part in raising the mindset and the consciousness of our society, through education, how we raise our children, the conversations we have, getting involved with grassroots organizations, being active, blogging, campaigning, becoming elected officials. When we do, the laws will change naturally. As we evolve, so will the world.

You may also be asking, "How is our life's purpose tied to love being everywhere?" Because God and the Universe are love, and our purpose here is to love, not just in romantic love but in all its forms. God's love is omnipresent. We are starting to see a new world emerging, with more messages of love and peace than ever before. We all need to be teachers in our own way to help transform this world away from fear and into love. We are living in a time that needs a lot of healing, and we are going to need everyone's help to step up to help heal this world together. With all our technological advancements, it's easy to think we live in a modern society, but we are still evolving as a human race. God's plan was not for us to be divided and to be separate from one another. His plan is for us to love and accept one another, and to live in unity in spite of our differences—racial differences, gender differences, sexual orientation differences, religious differences, etc. What separates us from each other, separates us from God. We are all his children. This world is our earthly home.

"There is no way to peace. Peace is the way."

~ A.J. Muste, Peace Activist

It's going to take a shift in the mindset of the world from fear to love to help bring the world's chaos into peace.

In yoga and meditation class, we often end class with this beautiful prayer:

Lokah samastah sukhino bhavantu

Which in Sanskrit means:

> "May all beings everywhere be happy and free and may the
> thoughts, words, and actions of my own life contribute
> in some way to that happiness and freedom for all."

Imagine if we all started and ended our day with this prayer, how different the world would be?

As you know, this is a relationship book and not a program on finding your life's purpose. That is an entire program in itself, but just as with many lessons in this book, it is the catalyst for a deeper practice, you may want to look into after you finish this book. As I said, I had many teachers after Gabby. So, this is just to plant a seed to get you started. You may not have picked up a book on life purpose, but your higher-self guided you to one through a relationship book.

If you want to learn more about life purpose, check out Eckhart Tolle's international best-selling book New Earth: Awakening Your Life's Purpose—an Oprah book club selection. Oprah maintains it's still one of her favorite books.

~ ~ ~

Your Path and Your Partner

*"I hope you find someone who speaks your language so
you don't have to spend a lifetime translating your spirit."*

~ Unknown

Once you find healing and become more consciously aware, this most likely will change the type of partner you're attracted to now. If it hasn't, start becoming aware of who and what you want to allow into your life and whether they are aligned with the new life you are creating. I know it has changed for me. As I've grown, what I want in a partner has changed as well. When I was in college, the only dating criteria I had was that he was cute and he was nice, maybe he drove a nice car. After I graduated and got my first job at a PR firm, my criteria changed. I was on the career track. I wanted a handsome, educated professional guy who came from a good family. Even though that sounds good on paper doesn't mean I made the right decisions for myself, as we all know, my marriage to the handsome professional guy who came from a good family ended in divorce because in the end we were such different people.

I still want many of those same things, but for me, I also want a partner who values personal growth, humanity, and wants to give back to the community in the same way I do. I want a partner, not just a boyfriend or a spouse. That doesn't mean he can't have his own interests, hobbies or opinions, but for me, we must be aligned. Nothing is harder than being in a relationship with someone who not only doesn't understand your vision, hopes, and dreams, but is against them. Nothing is better than being in a relationship with someone who supports your dreams.

Trust me, life is not only better, but easier with a partner who supports you. If you meet someone who is already disagreeing with your beliefs from the beginning, I can tell you right now, you're in for a long and rocky road together. Instead find someone who does support you and your dreams. If he doesn't, let him go without the fear of you being alone. Even if the chemistry is way hot, forget the passion. If he doesn't support you, he's not for you.

However, many people don't figure that out until they're three years into the relationship and the newness, fun, and the passion begin to wear off—and you find you're left in a empty relationship with someone who is not a match for you, or you for them. Hold out for a partner who wants to see you succeed and is in your corner, because someone who supports you and believes in you is way hotter in the long run. As you continue to evolve, you will naturally lose interest in people who you are no longer aligned with you. You no longer have the desire to win their approval or acceptance. You will also naturally attract people who are good for you and be more attracted to conscious people.

~ ~ ~

Love is All Around You. Really, it is!

Love is all around you! Really it is! You just have to open our eyes to it! As I mentioned earlier in this lesson, it can be found in the sky and in the trees. We spend so much of our free time distracted with our ear buds in our ears that even if you go out in nature, you're not connecting to its energy. Go out and connect with the love that's already around you, even if you live in the city like I do. Look for the smiles and love among people on the streets.

We were born to love and be loved. When we don't feel love, what it means is we have disconnected ourselves from Universal love, God's love, and from the truth. We have forgotten who we are and the light and love that already shines within us and we have defaulted back to ego. God never disconnects himself from us. The energy of love is always there, available to us at any time, waiting for us to connect ourselves back to it. And we can connect to this energy by noticing the love that is around us already. God is love, and love is his greatest gift to us. When we stop attaching the meaning that love only applies to a specific romantic kind of love, you will start seeing and feeling that love is all around you, and that love, all love, is love.

Finding love and the beauty all around you is much like the exercise we did on looking for everything with the color red. What we focus on is what we see. When we shift our focus on seeing more love in ourselves and out in the world, we start seeing more love in our lives. Love is in nature. It's in the flowers, water, and in the air we breathe. It's walking through the leaves or snow on a beautiful fall or winter day. Love is in our family, and it's in our friendships. It's also in the smiles of the strangers we meet. Love is in the nuzzle and purr of a cat. It's in the joy of a dog who found the best stick.

Love What You Do

Love can also be found in the things you do. Have you ever been so engrossed while doing something you love? You get lost in time. That is exactly how I feel as I write this book. I get to write about love all day. It's hard to be in a bad mood when you're writing about love.

Enjoying what I do makes life so much better. I look forward to my work. It takes a lot of sacrifice writing a book. I always took time out for self-care with daily walks along the bay and yoga, but I missed a lot of beautiful days and hanging out with friends, although it doesn't feel like a sacrifice when you love what you do.

Feed Your Soul

Do more of what feeds your soul. Even if for twenty minutes a day. "I don't have time," you may say. But you find time for Netflix binges, Facebook, and other time bandits. In life, if you want to get to where you want. It's going to take work, and either you make time, or find an excuse. Once you know what it's like to be connected versus being out of alignment, you do everything you can stay aligned.

Other ways I add more love through my day are through my yoga and meditation practice. If you're already a yogi and doing it, you know what an invaluable practice it is. Have I mentioned yoga and meditation in every lesson? And I am far from being an Instagram yogi. Yoga isn't about performance, but in how it connects you to self and helps to keep you aligned and centered. For me, on some days, yoga is about releasing, not relaxing, releasing what is not serving me, and asking the Universe to help me see it another way. Which I do very consciously and intentionally. On other days, it's about being grateful. Grateful for all that I have, and gratitude for this practice. Often both.

I also find love in cooking something fun and healthy, and creating something new. Find what feeds your soul and do more of it.

Believe in the Energy of Love

You must believe in the universal energy of love in order to connect to it. If you don't believe in it, it won't work for you. I always say, "practicality is the killer of dreams." Practicality and nay saying has killed more dreams than failure ever will. Because you kill the dream before even giving it a chance. Practicality, "I'm just being realistic," is the biggest excuse for fear. Fear of "what if it doesn't work out?" "Fear of what will people think of me?" "Fear of looking foolish." "Fear of

being let down." People who succeed don't focus on those things because they know it only holds you back.

Our beliefs control our perception, and our perception creates our reality. If you want to succeed in this, you have to believe that love is already all around you. If you feel that you do not have love in your life, you will believe you do not have love in your life. Remember, you do not lack love; you just haven't been tapping into its abundance. Then you have people who say, "Yeah, it feels good to connect, but I don't know? If it's working?" Stop questioning it! If you feel stupid doing it, you have to stop caring so much what other people think. If it feels stupid, you have to continue opening your mind to allow healing to work. Nothing will work unless you allow it to work. Now, is the time to take a stand to do what is good and right for you if it's working for you! You can connect to this energy every day by noticing all the love that is around you, or you can continue not to believe, because you're too smart for this, and remain where you were. The choice is always yours. However, know this energy is always available to you at any time to melt away feelings of lack or loneliness in your life and nurture and reenergize you with its loving presence.

Take a moment right now and put your hand on your heart and connect to the energy of love. Send yourself all of the love you need. Into every crevice and cell in your body. Breathe in and out of the space until you can really feel the energy all around you. Take as long as you need, then open your eyes. Pretty freaking amazing, isn't it? You are magic! That is the power you have within you. This is the difference between numbing activities that ego chooses, with fast, temporary fixes like casual sex and alcohol that can leave your soul feeling more depleted afterwards, versus love-based activities, love-based activities recharge your soul. Loved-based activities reenergize you, because you are tuning in, not tuning out. It is at these times we are most connected to our true selves and the energy of the Universe. Take time to really become aware of all the love and beauty around you every day. Really feel it and savor it. We have such an abundance of it! When you are full of love, you have enough loving energy now to send back out and share it with the world.

~ ~ ~

Being Wholeheartedly Single Around the Holidays
Yes! Love is Everywhere Even Around the Holidays!

Every day is the best day to practice love being everywhere, but one of the best times to utilize this practice is during the holidays. Many single people feel depressed around the holidays—Christmas, Hanukkah, Kwanzaa, and especially on Valentine's Day, a.k.a. "Single Awareness Day." That time of year is when singles feel most self-conscious about not having a partner.

First, it's a good time to remember that nothing has meaning unless we give it meaning. Take the meaning away or change its meaning, then what do you have? The answer is, something that no longer controls you. It's the same with holidays. They have no meaning other than the meaning and power you give it. Stop giving so much power to the feelings you don't want to have around the holidays, and focus more on how you do want to feel. If it's to feel love, remember you don't need a partner to feel love during the holidays, not even on Valentine's Day. The holidays are the best time to focus on the magic of the holidays. Don't allow your friends and relatives to refocus your energy back on negativity or lack. Once they stop picking up vibes from you, they will stop. Everything we feel is reflected back to us.

Also remember, not everyone who is in a relationship is happy either, but let's stay out of the habit of looking at someone else's unhappiness as our gain. But rather, let's remember that we were those people at one time too, and how it's much better to be single than to be in a bad relationship or even a relationship just to be in a relationship. Those are always so boring and annoying. And not fair to the other person if they are digging on you. Or worse they're just using you too. How sad is that? It's much better to learn to be on your own. Take this time to focus on your happiness and not what someone else can bring you. Keep in mind the type of relationship you want and not settling for less. Focus on what brings you joy, and not filler joy, which is, "This is what I am doing until I meet someone," but really tapping into "what brings me joy now." I find my joy walking along the bay every morning. People ask to come with me, but I like going on my own; connecting with nature and doing a walking meditation. I also love driving along the beach listening to great music or reading a good book in a quiet little café.

Maybe you don't realize it at the moment, because you've been with your family and friends forever and everything seems mundane, but truth is nothing stays the same. Family and friends will move away, and some will pass away. This is part of the ebb and flow of life. Cherish each and every moment now. Focus on the spirit of the holidays, giving to others, and all the love that surrounds you. Make it your mission to find and see love and joy everywhere unless you want to continue focusing on what you don't have and remain unhappy? That's your choice. Everything is a choice. But why be unhappy when you can be happy? Happiness is a choice. "What will you do to feel the way you want to feel?" That's from Danielle LaPorte's *Desire Map*. I love that.

I know it's almost impossible to fake happiness when you don't feel happy, but being unhappy is also not somewhere you want to stay for long periods of time. It's natural to feel unhappy once in a while due to circumstances. However, you don't want depression to become a way of life. For many, but not all, depression and negativity can be alleviated through this entire practice. You can begin rewiring your brain within 40-days for it to start taking longer-lasting effects. But like personal hygiene, we must take care of our mental well-being and thoughts every day at every moment before it takes over you. With regular practice, you will see a more loving world around you and less of what is lacking in your life.

An excellent way to reframe Valentine's Day is to think of it as a day of loving service. Patrice Tanaka and Company (PT&Co.), a PR firm I worked for in the West Village in New York City back in the day, wanted to expand the idea of Valentine's from romantic love to brotherly love. The agency even mailed out Valentine's Day cards to clients, family, friends and media to wish everyone a 'Happy Valentine's' and to inform them that the office would be closed that day so employees could commit, "Acts of Love and Kindness" in the community.

One day over afternoon tea at Bergdorf Goodman on Fifth Avenue overlooking Central Park, I was excited to share with Patrice, now a longtime friend and mentor, that I was including PT&Co.'s Acts of Love and Kindness campaign in this book. It was so interesting to hear Patrice reflect on the movement. She said, "We were very specific in noting these were not 'random acts.' There is nothing random about committing acts of love and kindness; acts of love and kindness are intentional." What a lovely approach to be more mindful about our acts of love and kindness.

I recall being encouraged to volunteer at a soup kitchen, or take an elderly relative or neighbor living alone out to lunch, visit a sick friend, or bake cookies for your children's class. You could do whatever act of love you could think of for that day. The day was yours to decide how you wanted to spend it. The following day, we all came back to the office discussing what acts of love and kindness we committed. Patrice also shared with me, how a former PT&Co. employee contacted her last Valentine's Day to give her a check for $10,000 to donate to the charity of her choice! It's evident that this campaign still lives on in the hearts of so many even after so many years. Patrice has since retired from agency life and started a new venture as the Chief Joy Officer of Joyful Planet LLC. Her mission is to help individuals and organizations discover and live their purpose to unleash greater success, fulfillment and joy in their personal lives, workplaces and communities.

To this day, Valentine's Day represents acts of love and kindness to me. What a gift that was, to no longer associate Valentine's Day with romance and cliché activities that bring everyone down even when you are in a relationship, if it's not perfect or ideal. It has now become a day of community, love, and service.

Be conscious of what gifts the Universe is trying to share with you. One of the key things in receiving your gifts is getting out of your own way, and knowing they may not always come in the form you expect them to be. Use the holidays to share, invite, and spread love. Help others, serve or even help change the perception of what Valentine's Day means to someone else who is still calling it "Single Awareness Day." Go out with your friends and family, and celebrate each other and love. Look for magic, and you will find it!

And know that when it's time, you will be celebrating and sharing the holidays and Valentine's Day with that amazing partner too, because they saw the joy in you. You'll be glad you didn't settle.

~ ~ ~

Connecting to Your Superpower

Intuition

In this lesson, you are going to learn how to connect to your super-power, aka, your intuition. Connecting to your higher-self or the Universe for guidance. Look at your intuition as your internal GPS. It not only guides you but also fuels your inspiration and creativity. Our strongest connection to this energy is through meditation, prayer, and our awareness of it will hone and cultivate it. Think of prayer as setting your intentions while meditation quiets the mind, so you can receive the answer through your intuition. Intuitive hits or "downloads" as we call them on this path, then start being delivered and channeled through you.

With a consistent meditation practice, you will be able to connect with source anytime. I know I am never alone when I stay connected to Source. Even on days I'm not feeling it, I know God is with me. If I feel disconnected, I know I just need to tap back into it. Connect back to Source when you are struggling and looking for support. When you feel unsupported, know it is because you stopped relying on the strength of the Universe and started using your own. When we connect with divine guidance through our intuition, it becomes your superpower.

Honing and Trusting Your Intuition

To start honing your intuition, all you have to do is start using it and trusting the guidance you receive. You may think you're crazy at first, but the more you use and trust it, the stronger it will get. Denying it and not trusting yourself, is what dulls your senses. This week we're really going to start using it and trusting it. What is intuition good for? Intuition is amazing for pretty much everything. As I said, it was the conduit for me writing this book. It guides me on my path.

Intuition is good for tapping into a situation with a friend or a loved one. If there has been some tension in an important relationship, instead of focusing on how right you are, tap into their perspective and ask what's really going on and what is the solution to resolve it so both parties are happy with the outcome? It can help you gain insight into the situation, if you are willing to see it through the lens of love. This can be tough to use in romantic relationships, because ego really blinds you in seeing things your way. So often we dismiss red flags because ego and your wounds, not your soul, doesn't want to see the red flags. When I got divorced, I joined a divorce support group. Pretty much everyone in the group said the warning signs were there, but they didn't listen to them. Start listening and trusting. It's there for your own good. Keep your eyes and mind open to the answers you receive, what it's truly trying to tell you. Red flags are intuition, however, fear is not. Be conscious of where you are being guided.

Fear vs. Intuition

A lot of people confuse fear and suspicion with intuition. It's not the same. Fear and suspicion can actually distort our perception a lot. Depending on how deep into the fear rabbit hole you've gone. Most of us know someone who is suspicious of everything or always worried about the worst-case scenario and truly believes it's for their own safety and protection or worse, your safety and protection. They always know best or at least their egos think they know best. Ego's perception is extremely convincing. Ego can bring up a lot of suspicion and fears when it is triggered, and it does think it's protecting you. There is an excellent anacronym for fear: *False Evidence Appearing Real*. Fear is an illusion that can significantly alter our perception into believing something is there that is not.

So how can you tell whether you are experiencing fear or intuition? When you are very upset, your heart is racing, and you are worrying, suspecting something terrible could happen, that is a good indication to dial it back a few notches and center yourself to get a better perception, because ego is leading you into fear. Intuition, on the other hand, is very calm and quiet. It could be something that would typically be upsetting to you, but you remain calm. You have a sense of "knowing." You may get upset once you find out you were right, but intuition itself is very calm.

Real world tip:

Intuition can get tricky when it comes to love. We see what we want to see. Let's say you are dating someone, and you become suspicious or triggered. You start thinking "It's been two days and he hasn't called," or "He canceled our date again at the last minute," or "Is he cheating?" or "Was he flirting?"

Then start thinking, "Oh, this must just be my ego. I need to calm down."

In truth, it may be your ego and you need to calm down, but above all else— above any triggers, fears, and ego, you deserve respect. Basically, if he likes or loves you, you will know. If he doesn't and you're just a fling or convenient, you'll be confused. It doesn't matter if it's the first date. A guy who respects you will never keep you waiting or wondering. Remember, healed resilient lovers don't fight for their worth; they know their worth. As always, find the balance.

~ ~ ~

Signs and Synchronicities

Signs and synchronicities are another way the Universe or your angels try to communicate with you. There is a lot of information out there in bookstores on signs and synchronicities, this is just a brief introduction. If you want to go more in-depth, I highly recommend my friend, Mary Soliel's book, *I Can See Clearly Now: How Synchronicity Illuminates Our Lives*. It's definitely one of my favorite books on the subject. You may have already encountered signs from the Universe, not knowing it actually was a sign from the Universe. Here are a few ways you can tell.

Signs

Signs are symbols and messages from our angel guides and the Universe. Signs can sometimes be just a "Hello" from your angels, reassuring you they are with you and you are loved and supported. These signs most often come in the form of a feather you find on the ground or your shirt. Signs can also be heart-shaped objects. It could be a heart-shaped cloud, puddle, or even a potato chip. It can even be the word "Love" seen in a store window or artwork on the street.

We can also assign symbols to our angels and the Universe. During my divorce, my symbol was a blue butterfly, which symbolized transformation, change, and that something new and beautiful would emerge. Whenever I saw a blue butterfly, I knew I was on the right path and that everything would be okay. Another sign for me are blue hydrangeas, my sister Marjorie's favorite color and flower. When she transitioned into heaven and became one of my angels. I know whenever I see blue hydrangeas now or hear one of her favorite songs, she is with me. I remember one day having lunch alone reading a book at my favorite cafe by the beach, *Jojo's Apple Cafe* in Point Lookout, NY. Two women stopped at my table and were talking about the beautiful painting hanging on the wall above me. I hadn't noticed it. I looked up, and it was a watercolor painting of blue hydrangeas. I knew it was my sister, wanting to get my attention to look at the painting I had missed. Another time when our mother was in the hospital, in front of the hospital were bushes of blue hydrangeas. I knew Marjorie was with me and my mom, at a time I felt alone. Other ways loved ones who have passed into heaven give us signs they are with us is through pennies on the ground. You may have heard of the old phrase "pennies from heaven." I tell you, no one finds more pennies than my mom. I think my sister knows that's mom's favorite way to know she is with us.

I swear, these things may sound crazy at first, but the more you put your focus on them, the more abundant they come. They're too wild to be coincidences. Now that you're focused on them, you'll start seeing them too and know what I mean.

Many people report seeing a red cardinal appear in their backyard shortly after a loved one has passed. A sign can come in many forms—printed on a teacup, a postcard, a porcelain statue, or even on your social media newsfeed. A cardinal is a message that your loved one is near.

Messages from the Universe can come intuitively through downloads, but they can also be sent through people. A friend may suggest a book or an event that could change your life. Always remember, what you want may not come in the form you were expecting. It's also important to let go of the outcome. Keep your eyes and your mind open on where you are being guided, and always acknowledge and be grateful to the Universe when it arrives.

In another scenario, let's say you're wondering if the person you are currently dating is good for you? All of a sudden, you start coming across articles in magazines or social media posts on "How to Spot Relationship Red Flags." That could be a sign from your angels warning you of what those red flags are so you notice them, or you may see the opposite, you may start seeing articles on, "Are You Self-Sabotaging Love?" or "How to Trust," depending on which applies to your situation and what your angels want you to know. Signs and messages can also come in the form of a song on the radio or even a song stuck in your head. It could be your angels or the Universe trying to tell you something or from a loved one thinking of you.

Signs can come in many shapes and forms. You can recognize them by the way they resonate deep inside of you and make you feel. People who have never received a sign before will tell me stories they experienced after a loved one has passed, "I know it was my dad reaching out to me to tell me he loved me and he's okay." You just know it is a sign. It's undeniable. It turns non-believers into believers. That is when intuition is the strongest. If you want to start seeing your own signs, stay open to receiving them, and you will start seeing them. Signs are around you all the time. If you don't understand a message, ask the Universe or your angels to send it again in another form that makes more sense to you.

Synchronicities

Synchronicities are what many people think are "coincidences." These are those moments when you are thinking of taking better care of yourself and eating healthier, and you want to take a class on nutrition, then all of sudden you hear a woman in your yoga class say, "I signed up for an amazing class on preventative medicine last night!" That was not a coincidence but a synchronistic event.

The Universe is lining you up in the direction of your path, giving you the green light and maybe showing you where to go. This is an example of something you are thinking about in your inner world, and it starts showing up in your outer world. I have been a little obsessed with the Beatles lately. I'm not sure why, but now I see Beatles things everywhere. I hear their songs, people I know are talking about the Beatles, I see them on the news, even new documentaries are coming out. They broke up fifty years ago, yet they are still everywhere. Because something gets in your focus, you'll start seeing it everywhere or the Universe is sending you more and more of it. That's how it works.

A synchronistic event can also be you thinking about a friend, and all of a sudden, they call you. This is also an example of how we are all connected. You thought about them, and intuitively they knew you were thinking of them and called you. Another synchronistic event that I see is that sometimes I will get a message downloaded to me that I am to share with people who follow me on social media, and I'll see other people posting the same message. It used to feel like other people would think I was stealing their material, until I realized that sometimes the Universe sends out group messages. Like group texts. I had to remember: Ego thinks there is competition when there isn't. In reality, we are all working toward the same goal—to help send love and healing to the world. There can't be enough messages about healing, love, forgiveness, and unity until we accomplish this goal.

Earlier on my path, if I sent out an intention, because I wanted to learn more about releasing ego and letting go, all of a sudden, a teacher I followed on social media, (whether it was Gabby Bernstein, Marianne Williamson or Deepak Chopra), would start talking about it. It always seemed to be exactly what I needed to hear. The more you tune in to this, the more surreal it gets. At times, I've felt like Jim Carrey's character, Truman Burbank in the movie *The Truman Show*. In *The Truman Show*, Truman has no idea that he is being watched by an audience and a team of producers. The producers provided Truman with whatever he needed. However, the team of producers in my case is the Universe, watching my every step, helping me along the way.

If there is an increase of synchronistic events that are aligned with something you are working toward, it means you are on the right path. Roadblocks in your path could be the Universe's way of trying to re-direct you toward something else. It may not mean abandoning the project altogether, but it could mean you are meant to go about it differently.

Always trust your gut, even if you think you are being led to something good, but for some reason, it doesn't feel right to you. You have to ask yourself whether this is resistance or your intuition telling you to go another way. I was looking to enroll in a coaching school to get my certification. I saw an advertisement for a free weekend coaching workshop. I thought, "This looks awesome! This is definitely a sign!" I went to the weekend event. There were at least two hundred people there. It was highly charged, motivating, and very professionally done. I felt great! However, at the same time, a couple of things were bugging me, but I chalked it up to fear and resistance, so I signed up. Coaching school is very expensive, and this course was a lot less. I thought if I liked it, I would sign up with a more expensive school if I needed it. I had just finished my level two spiritual training with Gabby Bernstein at Kripalu in the Berkshires in Massachusetts, when this course began. Gabby's course was amazing, but I still had this nagging feeling that something wasn't right with this new school I was starting.

All of a sudden, I received a message from one of my soul sister classmates from Gabby Bernstein's Masterclass. She noticed we were now both in this school together. I knew she was already a certified life coach (life coaches are always learning), so I asked her what she thought about this school. She flat out told me she didn't like it and was going to get her money back. I knew this was a clear sign from the Universe that I had been ignoring my gut feeling, so now they were sending somebody to tell me to get out. I was grateful that I was able to get my money back easily, but I felt lost because I wasn't sure where I was going next? Then, sure enough, the next steps appeared. A couple of days later, I learned about, iPEC (Institute for Professional Excellence in Coaching) from two other soul sisters, well-respected coaches who had both graduated from iPEC. Synchronistically, iPEC also happened to have a free weekend workshop coming up. It was more expensive than the other school, but by then, I was so committed to this path that I signed up. iPEC turned out to be the perfect course for me that complemented my style and work. Not once did I ever question if iPEC or Gabby Bernstein were right for me. It always felt right. Always follow your gut.

I just want to take a moment to mention again, that we all have different teachers that resonate with us. Ancient white-haired men with beards and robes are not better teachers than women who teach today. That's the ego-mind competing and stereo-typing again. There is no better or best. It needn't be complicated text. If a teacher is helping you, it doesn't matter if the work is scholarly or a self-published. It doesn't matter if they are helping one person or thousands of people, they are doing the work as they are being called to do.

~ ~ ~

Becoming Your Own Guru

In this final week of exercises, you will focus on observing your intuition to begin honing it as your own superpower and allowing your inner guru to come through. Start trusting your instincts and listen to what it's telling you. Follow where it is guiding you. You may be led down a path that looks different from everyone else, and that may seem scary at first, but it's what you're being called to do and why you are here, and in your heart you know this is true. This is where standing up to your fear of judgment and being firm in your authenticity will help strengthen you.

What does honing your intuition have to do with relationships? It will help to guide you into making the right decisions in choosing a partner, listening to those red and green flags. And in your relationships to help you resolve issues that may come up. Our intuition helps us greatly on this path. It is our navigation system. The more you use your intuition, instead of trying to figure everything out, the more you can use these divine tools to guide you along the way and direct you.

Love and Beauty Are All Around You!

Part of your assignment this week and every week here on out is to start living a beautiful, miraculous life, which means you are going to start recognizing all of the love, beauty and abundance already around you! Even in the quiet moments. Instead of turning on the radio or T.V. to distract or entertain you, eat your breakfast in silence. Take a moment to be mindful and really taste what you are eating and savor the flavors. As you are getting dressed, get excited about the start of a new day and all of the new opportunities in store for you. When you come home at night, even if after a tough day, relish being home in your sanctuary. Take time out for self-care, even if you can breathe in love and reconnect in silence for 10mins. Don't have a place to do it? Sit in your closet or bathroom to do it. Just do it. Be mindful of the meal you are cooking, cook with love, even if only for yourself. Start noticing and feeling all the love and beauty that is already around you. If you feel yourself disconnect from it, and you will. Witness it without judgment, and reconnect to it to keep the feeling and momentum going. Remember to ask yourself, "How do I want to feel today? What is going to get me there?"

Remember, it takes 40-days to retrain your brain to develop a new habit, so do this at least for 40-days to start incorporating a new way of being into your life. If you fall out of practice, get into the habit of not judging yourself, and pick up where you left off. It's more important to start again, than to blame yourself for not being perfect at something, and stopping altogether.

When we are in lack or in need, it means we have reverted back to our fear-based mindset, and the world will project that back to us. It's easy to miss all of the blessings already around us when you are viewing the world with your lack filters on. But ask anyone who has been sick for any length of time and they will tell you, just having your health every day is a blessing. Having food, running water and a roof over your head is also an enormous blessing.

If someone or something has a negative impact on you, say, "I choose to see this with love," detach and shake out the negativity. Listen to something inspiring. If you've been triggered, do the work, send love into those wounds, and heal them. Do everything you can to get yourself back to your peace, happiness, and love-based miracle mindset. If necessary, go back to any of the earlier lessons on forgiveness and self-love. Get used to doing this, because in your own practice, you will go back and forth quite a bit using these tools, sometimes several times a day, as you are releasing and up-leveling, all while continuing to keep moving forward. Once you get into the habit of it and know your tools, you will be reaching for them all the time, and being grateful for your practice. It's not as difficult as it sounds. Go easy on yourself and give yourself time. Remember, this is a practice, not perfection. Always accept where you are, while striving for more.

A love-based miracle mindset will not only help you attract more good things into your life, but you will also have a more beautiful and meaningful life along the way!

Love is Everywhere Exercises

Affirmation: "I see the love that is always all around me, when I open my eyes to it."

Love-is-everywhere song: "What a Wonderful World,"
Louis Armstrong

Pocket reminder: Your pocket reminder can be the words, "Love is everywhere."

Altar Prep

In your final week you will set up your altar with words and symbols about love being all around you.

Love Is Everywhere—Fun Photo Exercise!

Here is a fun exercise and mission. As you go through the week, take pictures of where the Universe is showing you love. This can be hearts in a store window, heart shaped clouds, even heart shaped gum on the sidewalk. Document the special signs you are receiving from the Universe. Take photos and share them in the Facebook group or with your friends on Instagram. Show the world the love signs you are receiving from your angels and the Universe. Hashtag #resilientlove to share and find other Resilient Lovers like you!

Get into the Love Groove with Music

If you are having trouble shifting into a loving energy, try getting into the mood with music. Normally, I don't recommend forcing a shift in your energy, because there usually is something to be revealed in that energy, instead of trying to always bypass it.

For the purpose of this week's lesson, we will use music as a tool to get into our love groove or to shift our energy and vibration. Just like thoughts, music can do so much to evoke our emotions. What we listen to reinforces our moods. Find music that will lift you up and makes you feel empowered and joyful.

Day 1: Love-is-Everywhere Exercise: Intuition

Start using your intuition this week.

- What's coming up for you? What is your intuition, your higher love-based self, telling you about a particular situation?

  Become aware of whether you are being triggered or if there are any ego/fear beliefs around your situation. Remember, suspicion is not your intuition. Ego is slick and can make you assume fear-based beliefs that are not true.

  We always have a choice to see things differently. We always have a choice to see through the lens of love, instead of through the lens of fear, anger, and worry. When you see through the lens of love, you are seeing through your higher-self. You are seeing with love and understanding. Your ego may think this is a weakness and prevent you from working things out, but your higher-self knows this is strength and will create more connected and loving experiences in your life. What is your higher-self telling you?

  Get into the habit of asking yourself, "What am I to learn from this? What is the opportunity here?"

- Or where is your higher-self guiding you? Where are you feeling inspired to go, create or share? If you don't know, ask. Remember not to worry, if it doesn't come to you right away. It sometimes can take time, but once you set the intention out there, know and trust it will be answered in some shape or form. It may not be how you expected, so stay open.

Repeat these steps every day or as often as necessary.

Altar

Meditation • Prayer • Intention

Go to your altar and set up words and inspiration for this week with the word "love" and what it means to have love all around you. Light the candle and meditate. Connect to your higher-self and Source energy.

When I want to connect to inspiration and source, I send the energy from my higher-self all the way up, up, up, to connect with the God and the Universe above.

When I need healing or loving energy, I picture golden white light, falling all around me and into the spaces that need healing. I allow the loving energy to come through each time I inhale, giving it permission to transform me while exhaling all that loving energy back into the world.

Day 2: Love-is-Everywhere Exercise: Look for Signs

Today and from this day forward, start looking for love signs and signs from the Universe.

They could be signs based on something you are seeking an answer on. Set your intention on where you want guidance, and be open for the answer to come in many forms, such as an article, a conversation you overhear, a friend, a song, or as a download through your intuitive thoughts. The more receptive you are to your intuitive thoughts, the more downloads you will receive.

Be open to receiving signs of love that the Universe is sending you. This could be hearts, the word "love," pennies, feathers, repetitive numbers, and your spirit animals. Share your findings with the Resilient Love Facebook group.

Altar

Meditation ▪ Prayer ▪ Intention

Light the candle. Say a prayer or meditate. Sit in easy pose and close your eyes. Clear and release anything that is on your mind. Breathe and get centered. Try listening to Tibetan bells. You can find videos on YouTube. Tibetan bells are really good to use for silent meditation. Focusing on the tone of the bell fading in and out clears your mind, allowing your intuition to come through stronger. Meditate from 7 to 20 minutes. Longer, if you so desire. Set an intention before you meditate on something you want clarity on, or an answer for and wait for the answer to come through. Meditation quiets the mind to allow messages to come through.

Day 3: Love-is-Everywhere Exercise: Feel and See Love All Around You

Today and every day, incorporate signs and be open to the love that is already all around you, all of the time. It may feel silly to some of you at first, but once you get into the practice not judging yourself and caring what other people think, it will feel a heck of lot better than having your guard up all the time, being cynical, and feeling like crap. This practice will set you free.

Start recognizing that love is in the air; it's in the flowers, trees, and in the grass when you walk and connect with nature. It's in the big blue sky and ocean waves. It's in the things you do every day, that first sip of coffee, or reading a book in quiet little café. It's taking a walk on a beautiful quiet snowy day or rustling your feet through leaves on a fall day. Love is doing what brings you joy. It's riding a bike, cooking a healthy meal, painting or drawing, or writing from your heart. Be mindful of these moments instead of living a life distracted through out the day, but rather take in the loving energy, and allow it to move and flow through you.

Love is also in the people on the streets. Love is in the smile and laughter between friends, between a parent and child, between lovers, and in an old lady's smile. Every time you see their joy, know that their joy is there for you to enjoy. I know it can sometimes be hard to get into this space when you're just not feeling it. Remember to monitor your thoughts, because they are a direct reflection of how you are feeling. Get serious about letting go of what is not serving you. And have the willingness to choose to see love over what you are feeling. And keep surrendering as often as needed. Continuing to show up for yourself makes all the difference.

Continue staying connected to Source energy, finding the love in your meditation, yoga practice, or any activity you do that feeds your soul and connects you to the love in and around you. Savor and be mindful of living in the moment.

Altar

Meditation ▪ Prayer ▪ Intention

Light the candle. Say a prayer or meditate. Clear and release anything that is in your mind first. Breathe and get centered. Connect to the love all around you. Do a minimum of 7 to 20 minutes per day.

Or listen to your bonus "Love is Everywhere" meditation I created for you on my website at:

- karenom.com/resilient-love-meditations
- Password: resilientlover

Day 4: Love-is-Everywhere Exercise: Find More Love in Your Friendships

This is one of my favorites! And a life changer for me. Today and every day moving forward, find more love in your friendships and with your family. Find the love, joy, and special moments in your relationships with them. Spend time making memories and making each moment count. You're not just killing time with them until you find "the right one." If these relationships are special to you, relish them and treat them special. When you are together with your friends and family, refrain from talking about why you haven't met someone yet and how much that sucks. Instead, talk about the beauty of life, what inspires you, your passions, what's meaningful and important to you, what you want to create, what you can do to make the world a better place? Talk about what kind of partner that would fit into your new inspired life. Make a conscious effort to be present. Appreciate the love and connection every time you are together.

Altar

Meditation ▪ Prayer ▪ Intention

Light the candle. Say a prayer or meditate. Clear and release anything that is in your mind first. Get centered and think about all the loving friendships and relations you have in your life. Be grateful. Do a minimum of 7 to 20 minutes.

Day 5: Love-is-Everywhere Exercise: Love is Service

You do not need to do this exercise if Service is not resonating with you at the moment. Don't judge yourself if you are not feeling called right now. Instead, you can repeat any exercise from Days 1 through 4.

- We all have a purpose here on Earth if we choose. What do you feel called to do?
- What healing practices are you most passionate about?
- Health and nutrition, mental wellness, yoga, meditation, mindfulness, reiki, spreading more love and kindness, unity, bridging divides?
- What issues today are important to you: Helping the homeless, helping people in recovery, empowering the poor, animal rights, helping sexual assault victims, women empowerment? Bringing more healing into the world? There are so many to choose from.
- What are your gifts? What is unique about your gifts?
- What have you always wanted to do, but have been too afraid or never made time to do?
- What would it feel like to start doing it? What steps can you take?
- How could the world benefit from you stepping out of your comfort zone and sharing your gifts?
- How is owning your voice, allowing yourself to be heard, and sharing your gift all acts of love?

If you are not sure how to share your gifts? You can bring awareness on social media, blogs, public speaking, or writing a book. It could even be through running empowerment or mindfulness groups or volunteering in your community.

There are so many ways we can serve. Start sharing your message or the progress you've made on your journey. Share with friends, family, and co-workers. Sharing on social media is one of the best ways to get your message out. It's your page and your voice. If your

messages come from your heart, people will be less reactive, but not everyone will love it or agree. This is where you start standing in your authentic voice.

Even if it serves one person, you made a difference to that one person. But you will be surprised by how many people you impact who do not say anything. Then all of a sudden, you will get that message in your inbox, or you will see someone in public who will say, "Your posts have really helped me," or "Your posts make my day." This is how we share and spread the light.

Start your day with the three prayers provided in this lesson. If you haven't done so already, make it part of your daily practice. They are life-changing and will help you maintain and create a more meaningful life and a miraculous, loving mindset.

Be open and ready to receive your inspirations. You can share something or create something. A beautiful Instagram post, or write something that will help someone else feel healing or inspired through your words. What is your transformational healing story? What modalities changed your life? What issues today do you feel passionate about? Really feel connected to the loving energy as you do it. Allow the Universe's divine energy to guide you and speak through you. Embrace this sacred time, being connected to Source.

When people ask me how I stay connected and inspired, I share this process. I write about something I am passionate about, which is one of my favorite ways to stay connected and inspired. It also keeps the creative juices flowing. The more I write, the more ideas are given to me. Taking workshops and listening to audiobooks about spiritual growth keeps me connected and inspired as well.

Seek opportunities and face your fears. Don't let the voice of ego win. It is going to tell you, "Should I share this? What are other people going to think?" Squash ego's voice and share your authentic, loving voice. I will note: only share what you are ready to share. Don't share from your wounds, but from your healing. Release your attachment to validation on how many "Likes" you got and focus on how brave you are that you shared it, even if no one likes it. The more you do it, the more comfortable you will feel in sharing your true voice. Every level is going to require a different version of you. Just keep moving a little further to overcome your fears at a pace that feels comfortable, but keep it at a consistent pace. You may need to hire a coach, attend workshops, and read many books to keep moving forward and elevating. Connect with someone you admire and ask them what steps they took that helped them get where they are. Speak up!

Surround yourself with like-minded people. Find an accountability partner or a spiritual running buddy. If you can't find people locally, that is the magic and the gift of the internet. Connect with like-minded people online who inspire each other to grow. When you surround yourself with like-minded people, you will have a greater chance of achieving your goals because they will inspire you to grow and keep going. Don't let ego compare you to others or make you feel behind. Their journey is not your journey. You are on your own path, and you are right where you are supposed to be. The point is to keep moving forward, no matter what ego barriers get in your way. If you continue this way, a year from now, you will be a lot closer to reaching your goal than if you didn't try at all.

Altar

Meditation • Prayer • Intention

Light the candle. Say a prayer or meditate. Clear and release anything that is in your mind. Breathe, get centered, and allow the loving energy to come through and inspire you on your purpose. Do a minimum of 7 to 20 minutes. Pay attention after you meditate on what is coming through for you. Some people get intuitive hits during meditation, and some people get it after, as they are going about their day.

Day 6: Love-is-Everywhere Exercise: Being in the Flow of Universal Love

Today, you are going to connect with divine energy of the Universal love within you. Just practice being the energy of love. Feeling the energy move through you, and radiating that love back out into the world, becoming a part of the Universal flow of loving energy. You are the love and light within you. You are at one with the divine love and energy of the Universe.

Send that loving, healing energy to people as you walk by. Be kinder, smile at people, hold doors, let someone in line with more groceries cut in front of you, compliment, or have a friendly chat with stranger. If you are in a group, and you see someone alone, be more inclusive and ask them to join the group. Get out of your comfort zone if you're shy, stop caring what other people think. Lead by example. Lead with love. Do anything that spreads more love, healing, and unity into the world.

Altar

Meditation ▪ Prayer ▪ Intention

Light your candle. Use your essential oils. This is such a beautiful part of the practice. Say a prayer or meditate. Focus on clearing and releasing anything that is in your mind that no longer serves you. Breathe, get centered, and allow for the loving energy and white light to move through you. Do a minimum of 7 to 20 minutes, or you can do the Metta Prayer.

Metta Prayer

Place both hands on your heart.
Breathe slowly and deeply.

On the first round, you will breathe loving energy into your heart,
filling up your body.
    And say to yourself,
    May I be happy.
    May I be safe.
    May I live in peace.
    Repeat two times.

For the second round, send the loving energy you have created out to
those you love who need healing.
    And say to yourself,
    May you be happy.
    May you be safe.
    May you live in peace.
    Repeat two times.

On the third round, send the loving energy you have created to
people you may have judged or feel some adversity around. Knowing they only want the same things as you, to be loved, accepted and
understood.
    And say to yourself,
    May you be happy.
    May you be safe.
    May you live in peace.
    Repeat two times.

For the fourth round and final round, send this loving energy you have created out to everyone in the world. The world needs so much love and healing.

And say to yourself,

May you be happy.

May you be safe.

May you live in peace.

Repeat two times.

You may close by saying the Sanskrit mantra:

"May all beings everywhere be happy and free, and may the thoughts, words, and actions of my own life contribute in some way to that happiness and to that freedom for all."

~ Namaste

Day 7

Congratulations!! You did it! You have reached the final assignment in *Resilient Love Turn Your Wounds into Your Wings. Book One: Healing.* I hope this experience was as amazing for you as it was for me, and that you received the massive shifts I did on this journey!

Your final assignment is to celebrate yourself! Reflect on all the great work you have done and the amazing shifts you have created! You are officially a Resilient Lover!

How are you going to celebrate yourself today?

How are you going to share your beautiful self out into the world?

~ ~ ~

My Commitment and Pledge to Myself to Stay Resilient in Love.

I, _____, pledge ...

✓ To always love, honor, and respect myself first.
✓ To remember that God created me perfect. I am beautifully whole and complete as I am.
✓ To practice self-love daily, even if it's just accepting where I am today.
✓ To accept who I am and where I am in my journey and to forgive myself on days I don't.
✓ To choose to live from love and passion and not my fears.
✓ To add more joy into my life, knowing I am worthy.
✓ To live life more from a loved-based mindset, which sets me free and aligns me with my true path.
✓ To know relationships are assignments, teaching me how to love and honor myself and others more.
✓ To know as I heal, I elevate myself and my standards, and the Universe will meet me there.
✓ To know I am the gatekeeper of who I allow into my life.
✓ To trust myself to release anything that does not serve my highest good—setting boundaries is an act of self-love.
✓ To always pray to my highest self and for the highest good of all.
✓ To keep my heart open, and by keeping my heart open, I am showing the Universe my willingness to love and be loved.
✓ To know my practice in self-love, compassion, and forgiveness keeps me Resilient in Love. <3

Book Preview
Resilient Love Book Two:
Moving Forward

*T*HE NEXT BOOK IN the Resilient Love series (check my website at karenOM.com for the release date) is *Resilient Love: Moving Forward & Opening Your Heart to Love Again. Knowing how to recognize the right guy (and the wrong ones)* is the working title, will help you to learn how to empower yourself in dating and relationships so your ego doesn't take you out. You will continue to develop your awareness on how to keep your heart open to love, and learn how to recognize unhealthy partners before you get involved and give your heart to them, so navigating the dating scene won't seem as scary. It will be like having extrasensory perception when it comes to love and dating.

Everything we've been taught by society on how to meet partners is contrary to what is necessary to develop a healthy relationship, which is why the divorce rate is so high. If you want a long-lasting relationship, you can't get advice from dating experts on the singles' scene who have no idea what it's like to be married or what it takes to make a marriage work. There's a lot that happens after you get the guy (or girl).

This book will teach you how to better identify the people who have what it takes to make a relationship work, so you won't be dating in the dark when you learn how to put a light on it. Of course, you won't know everything about them, but you'll have a better idea of who is worth your time and who isn't. You won't have to rely on whether you can trust them to have your back, because you'll have your back.

Staying on the Path: Recommendations

Books

- *Universe Has Your Back*, Gabby Bernstein
- *Rising Strong*, Brene Brown
- *Self-Compassion*, Kristen Neff
- *Whatever Arises Love That, Matt Kahn*
- *Untethered Soul, Michael Singer*
- *Radical Self-Acceptance*, Tara Brach

Audiobook

- *The Power of Vulnerability*, Brenè Brown
  (only available on audio)

Meditations

- Oprah and Deepak Twenty-One-Day Meditation Series

Meditation/Yoga Music Albums

- "Expansive Spirit," Jai-Jagadeesh
- "Embrace," Deva Premal
- "Sanctuary," Donna DeLory
- "Sharanam: Sacred Chants of Devotion," Sudha & Maneesh
  de Moor

Stay Connected!

YOU CAN WORK WITH Karen OM individually in private one-on-one sessions or check her website and social media pages for upcoming group and online courses.

Website: karenOM.com

Facebook: https://www.facebook.com/karen.om30

Facebook Group: This is a private closed group for readers of *Resilient Love*. There, you can share your story, your amazing shifts and signs, and ask questions from other Resilient Lovers. Search in the FB search bar to locate the Resilient Love Book Club. Send a private message with the code: "I am a Resilient Lover" for access.

Instagram: https://www.instagram.com/karen.om_resilient.love/

Acknowledgements

_T_o God, my guiding angels, and the Universe who stood by me, worked through me every step of the way, and gifted me this book as my contribution to serving the world. Thank you <3

To my Soul Fam, who inspire me to show up every day. Because you guys show up every day, you encourage me to do the same.

To Irene Lovric, who listened to me for countless hours and helped to bring me back home. Thank you <3

To my beta testers. You guys contributed so much to this book to help make it what it is today. Thank you <3

To my life coach Anna Weaver, who did exactly what I hired her to do—get me to the other side—and who also listened to me for hours with love and compassion, and without judgement. I would also not be here without you.

To Peri Sedigh, one of my dearest and oldest childhood friends. Thank you for being the funnest and funniest, wonderful, supportive, and loving friend that I could ask for. And your part in helping to make this book happen.

Made in the USA
Middletown, DE
09 August 2020